Dancing

WITH

Diana

Dancing

WITH

Diana

A MEMOIR BY

ANNE ALLAN

**SUTHERLAND
HOUSE**

TORONTO, 2024

Sutherland House
416 Moore Ave., Suite 304
Toronto, ON M4G 1C9

Sutherland House and logo are registered
trademarks of The Sutherland House Inc.

First edition, September 2024

If you are interested in inviting one of our authors to a live event or
media appearance, please contact sranasinghe@sutherlandhousebooks.com
and visit our website at sutherlandhousebooks.com for more information.
We acknowledge the support of the Government of Canada.

Manufactured in Turkey
Cover designed by Lena Yang
Book composed by Karl Hunt

Library and Archives Canada Cataloguing in Publication
Title: Dancing with Diana : a memoir / by Anne Allan.
Names: Allan, Anne (Dance teacher), author.
Identifiers: Canadiana (print) 20240389239 | Canadiana (ebook) 20240389255 |
ISBN 9781990823893 (hardcover) | ISBN 9781990823909 (EPUB)
Subjects: LCSH: Allan, Anne (Dance teacher) | LCSH: Diana, Princess of Wales,
1961-1997. | LCSH: Dance teachers—Great Britain—Biography. |
LCSH: Dance teachers—Canada—Biography. | LCSH: Dance—
Great Britain. | LCGFT: Autobiographies.
Classification: LCC GV1785.A45 A3 2024 |
DDC 792.802/8092—dc23

ISBN 978-1-990823-89-3
eBook 978-1-990823-90-9

Contents

CONTENTS

CHAPTER ONE

The Phone Call

MY STORY STARTS in 1981, after the wedding of the century, and shortly before the beginning of my time with Princess Diana. It was September.

I was sitting down for a quiet evening at home after a long day of rehearsal for the London City Ballet on the second act of *Swan Lake*, the "white act," as it is known. I've always loved performing in that beautiful classic. It is the purest form of ballet. I was one of the "Big Swans." The name "Big Swans" has always made me laugh for the image it conjures, but the swans represent both power and support to the Swan Queen, and each role calls for a tall dancer.

Swan Lake is a romantic tale of love. Princess Odette and her friends have been turned into swans by the evil Von Rothbart. They spend their days swimming on a lake of tears, and their nights in human form. Prince Siegfried, while out hunting, sees the swans and falls in love with Odette, Queen of the Swans. At first, she is frightened of him. He discards his bow and promises never to harm her and to break the spell she is under. The curse can only be released by the power of ever-lasting love.

Later, at a costume ball at the palace, the disguised Von Rothbart introduces his daughter, Odile, to the prince. Thinking that she is Odette, the prince promises to marry her, only to later realize the terrible mistake he has made. Returning to the lake, he begs forgiveness from Odette, but it is too late. She sacrifices her life. Prince Siegfried takes his own life, uniting them forever.

The swans with their grace and beauty symbolize purity and faithfulness. Just like real swans, who mate for life.

My body was tired after the long day. The role demands incredible stamina, all those jetés diagonally across the stage area, perfectly in sync with the other dancers. I was glad to be at home in my cozy Highgate flat. I had just put my darling four-year-old daughter, Emily, to bed and was ready to sit down and put up my feet. At that precise moment, the telephone rang.

Emily was not the best sleeper in the world and the idea of her waking up spurred me to sprint to the phone. I never understood why our only phone line was in the bedroom next to hers on the shared wall. I had chosen her room for the beautiful tree outside the window, its leaves at the same level. She loved to look at them from her bed. We had to climb a metal staircase round the back of the house to get to the flat, but we loved that it was high up.

Grabbing the phone in hope that Emily hadn't heard it, I said hello in a very quiet voice. I pulled the phone cord into the hallway so I could sit at the top of the stairs, relieved that I hadn't heard a cry. The voice at the other end of the phone spoke in a very British upper-class voice. "Hello, this is Anne Beckwith-Smith, lady-in-waiting to the Princess of Wales."

I said, "Oh, hello," as one does, secretly thinking, *who the hell is this?* My mind raced to which friend had been put up to this prank.

But the posh accent continued talking. "The Princess would like to take dancing classes," she said.

"Oh," I said, still trying to work out what exactly was going on.

Over the next few seconds, as Anne Beckwith-Smith continued to speak, I had began to remember that something like this might happen but couldn't remember the details.

"Anne, could we please meet to discuss?" she continued.

I found myself saying, "Yes, of course."

"Let's meet at The Ritz on Friday if that suits you, Anne," she said, and suggested a time.

This was still sounding suspicious. The Ritz!

Bewildered, but not want to appear rude, on the off chance this was genuine, I agreed to meet without even thinking how the timing would work.

Anne then added in a rather official voice, "If you could please keep this conversation highly confidential, thank you."

Her tone stopped me in my tracks. I had no option other than to say, "Of course!"

I put the phone down, feeling a bit stunned, a flood of emotional reactions hitting me.

Was this real?

How would this work?

What dancing does she like?

Is this a hoax?

Why the intrigue?

As I sat on the stairs, details of a previous conversation came back to me. It had taken place on July 29, 1981. A day that made history.

I was both a dancer and the ballet mistress for the London City Ballet. Harold King was the artistic director. He, along with Marian St. Claire and Michael Beare, had founded the company and had arranged a beautiful day where all of us would join together to watch on television the celebration of the marriage of Prince Charles and Lady Diana Spencer. It was most unusual for ballet dancers to have an additional day off, but since this was a bank holiday, we were delighted at the extra rest from our usual schedule.

The atmosphere of celebration was everywhere in the country. There were street parties, family get-togethers, and much jubilation. We were about to watch Lady Diana become the newest member of the royal family, bringing with her a sense of hope for the future. We dancers sipped champagne together as we watched the day's celebrations, along with millions of viewers in countries around the world.

Before things got underway, Harold asked to speak to me privately for a few minutes in the kitchen. I joined him, thinking it was company-related. He told me that he, as well as a few other artistic directors, had been approached by Buckingham Palace—yes, *that* palace—to recommend dance teachers for Lady Diana. She was interested in taking dance lessons. He had put forward my name among others, and the list had now been whittled down to three candidates, of which I was one.

That day, at that time, right before the wedding celebration, right before I was to rejoin my company to celebrate, was the first I heard of any of this. I was honoured, and thanked Harold for thinking of me. I noticed myself watching the wedding with an extra layer of fascination.

The streets were lined with thousands of spectators, all the way from Buckingham Palace and Clarence House, where Lady Diana would leave from, to St. Paul's Cathedral, a masterpiece designed by Sir Christopher Wren in the late 1600s. We discussed the outfits of the 2,500 invited guests and were delighted on the arrival of the five brides-maids, who gave us just a hint of what the bride's dress might look like.

Carriages filled with royalty arrived before the glass fairy-tale coach that held Lady Diana, the future Princess of Wales. There was so much dress that she appeared to have had difficulty getting out of the coach. Although the dress had gotten a little wrinkled, once it had enough space to open up fully, we could see that it was stunning. It was made from ivory silk taffeta, decorated with antique lace, which was embroidered with sequins and pearls. The contours were like a crinoline, with puffy sleeves and a modest neckline. A gold horseshoe had been hidden in the dress for luck, and she wore her family's heirloom tiara with the veil. The cascading bouquet of gardenias, stephanotis (a symbol of happiness in marriage), freesias, and lily of the valley was exquisite. When she made her way up the stairs to the cathedral with her father, the magnificent twenty-five-foot train trailing behind her left us all breathless and teary-eyed.

We were breathless again during her three-minute walk down the aisle to begin her future. When she mixed up the order of Prince Charles's names during her vows, we thought it was endearing that her nerves were showing through. It seemed to make her very human.

By the time we got to the famous kiss on the balcony of Buckingham Palace, the public was well into its love affair with Diana, now Her Royal Highness the Princess of Wales. As I watched, I found myself thinking how absurd and improbable it would be that she would take dancing classes. I put the idea out my head and enjoyed the rest of the day. It seemed so unlikely that anything would come of my conversation with Harold that I promptly forgot about it.

And now, having just ended my phone call with Anne Beckwick-Smith, lady-in-waiting, I considered whether the conversation was, in fact, "the real McCoy," or "the real MacKay," as we say in Scotland. That brought on a mild panic.

Perhaps they are meeting with all the dance teachers who were under consideration. So, it could just be an interview? That brought a bit of relief. But, then, she didn't say that . . . but it would make sense.

I went through the rest of the evening like a zombie. When my husband came home, I didn't tell him about the mysterious call. One, because I had been told to keep it highly confidential, and two, I was worried about looking stupid when it turned out to be a joke. You must admit, it would have been funny.

CHAPTER TWO

The Meeting

I T WAS A long week after the Monday phone call. I kept replaying our short, mysterious conversation in my head in search of some definitive conclusion. Why had I been called at 8 p.m. and not during business hours? Was that suspicious? Could it have been someone impersonating Anne Beckwith-Smith and that's why it was such a short-and-to-the-point call? Again, were there other candidates meeting her?

Our inner dialogues can be ridiculous, so I was thankful that we were in intense rehearsals for *Swan Lake*. I decided to put my energy there. I was beginning to feel more in control of the "Big Swan" variation, gaining more strength every day as I worked on it.

I also stepped into my role as ballet mistress, in which I shared responsibilities for rehearsals with the ballet master, Michael Beare. I learned as much when rehearsing with the company as I did when I danced my role. I could see what was required visually as ballet mistress but, as a dancer, I could feel the technique required in my own body. To me, being a ballet mistress was like an extension of teaching, and I've always loved teaching. I started at a very young age as an assistant to

Margaret Hopkins, my ballet teacher in Glasgow. She was eighty-two years old when I left to go to London, just before my seventeenth birthday. I often trained with her on a one-to-one basis. She was endlessly patient and taught me as much about life as she did about dance and teaching.

Friday finally rolled around.

The meeting was at 11 a.m. Fortunately, I wasn't needed till the afternoon rehearsal that day, which was a stroke of luck, as I had agreed to the meeting without knowing the schedule. This meant I could take my daughter to kindergarten, attend my curious meeting, be back in time for afternoon rehearsal, and then pick her up again. I felt a surge of excitement and nervousness at the thought of the meeting and, still thinking it might be a hoax, got myself ready.

I had rummaged through my closet to find something suitable to wear. I thought I should look smart going to The Ritz and potentially meeting a lady-in-waiting. *Who exactly was a lady-in-waiting*, I found myself thinking. *What do they do?* I had very little idea. It appeared from television clips that they collected bouquets of flowers from the Princess or the Queen when they were given too many to carry.

I would learn later that there was much more to it. They are very proficient organizers of all the daily activities connected to the royal personage they serve, including secretarial tasks, dealing with correspondence on their behalf, and all etiquette connected to key engagements, including having background knowledge for every important guest who is being presented at an event. They usually come from aristocratic backgrounds and act as close companions, but their main qualities are having high moral standards and discretion.

There have been many notable ladies-in-waiting in history, including "The Four Marys"—Mary Seaton, Mary Fleming, Mary Beaton, and Mary Livingston—who joined a young Mary, Queen of Scots on her trip to France, and returned with her to Scotland after she was widowed. Anne Boleyn was a lady-in-waiting before becoming a wife of Henry VIII, and we all know what happened to her! Lady Anne Glenconner was a very close confidante to Princess Margaret from 1971 until the Princess died in 2002. And, most recently, there was Lady Susan Hussey, who served Queen Elizabeth II for decades. After Queen Elizabeth's death, she was made a Lady of the Household, serving in that position for a brief time before having to resign in late 2022, at the age of eighty-three, after making racist comments to Ngozi Fulani, a charity founder who was attending an event at Buckingham Palace.

Today, I would have quickly googled Anne Beckwith-Smith to do my research and have knowledge of her, but it was 1981 and that was not available to me. I'd seen a few news items regarding the Princess on television or in newspapers and had an idea of what Anne Beckwith-Smith looked like. Otherwise, I was in the dark. Anne had said, "Let's meet in the foyer," and I had agreed. Would I recognize her? Would she recognize me?

I walked from my Highgate flat to Archway tube station, where I got a tube to Piccadilly Circus. As I came up from the underground, in the heart of London, there it was, with its iconic façade, The Ritz, *not* The Ritz Hotel. I thought this said something about the brilliance behind the mind of the original Swiss hotelier, César Ritz, who created this masterpiece in 1906. I loved walking into the building, filled with a thrill at the thought of all the famous people, from politicians, film stars, rock stars, and royalty, who had walked through its revolving doors. I had read somewhere that Anna Pavlova, the renowned ballerina, had danced there in 1912. I loved knowing that. It made me feel a small sense of belonging.

I had only visited The Ritz once before, when I was in my final year at the Royal Ballet School. My friend and I had gone for afternoon tea in the Palm Court in celebration of our final year at school. I was nineteen. Naturally, this was the most wonderful memory as I had never experienced anything like it, being a wee girl from Glasgow, who had come to London on scholarship to train at one of the best ballet schools in the world. I remember I was blown away by the magnificent decor as we entered and how we felt so grown up and elegant as we floated to our table, passing the exotic palm trees, our faces beaming, knowing this was the treat that we had saved up for.

I hadn't wanted to be too early for the impending meeting so as not to look like a lost soul if no one was there. I had timed my entrance for five to eleven, like any good performer being prepared before entering the stage. After a few deep breaths, I walked through the foyer, my antenna alert.

A woman who was sitting at one of the white linen–covered tables immediately stood and came toward me with a bounce in her step. She extended her hand as she said, "How lovely to meet you, Anne. I'm Anne Beckwith-Smith, lady-in-waiting to Her Royal Highness the Princess of Wales. I thought it had to be you!"

I was relieved but did wonder how she knew it was me. It wasn't until years later that I realized she probably had a photograph of me and knew much more about me than I knew about her. There had probably been a background check conducted without my knowledge. I was unaware of those things at the time.

"We are both Annes," she said with a jolly laugh, inviting me to sit down at the table to have tea. Her personality was warm and inviting and made me feel very comfortable. "Tea sounds lovely," I said, thankful that I didn't have to order food and risk choking during the conversation.

The term "Sloane Ranger" popped into my head as the best way to describe Anne. Sloane Ranger was an expression of its day that implied the lady was upper class and lived near Sloane Square, an area of Chelsea well known for its wealthy residents. They would gravitate to their country homes at the weekend, wearing their blazers, tweeds, and brogues (but with pearls and scarves on hand) to enjoy horse riding or polo. Usually, they had private school education before entering public relations or working for charity organizations. Often, they studied fine art. "Preppy" would be the closest term in North America.

After a few minutes of polite exchanges and easy chat while waiting for the tea to arrive, she said without hesitation, "The Princess would like to take private dancing lessons with you."

I said, "How lovely," trying to keep calm, as the realization hit me that she had said "with you." This was not an interview.

"What kind of dancing does the Princess like and want to do?" I asked, trying to keep myself calm.

"Well, it's not so very clear to me, but she likes all that kind of modern dance and jazzy-type dance, whatever that is!" she said, laughing. "And, of course, she loves ballet."

At the time, I remember thinking *here is a very nice lady who doesn't know very much about different styles of dance*, but why should she? She probably knew a lot more about horses than I did.

I asked where the classes would take place. My ballet mistress mind raced to the necessity of a suitable studio with a sprung floor. I felt sure Kensington Palace didn't have one, and the idea of going there was too daunting anyway. Before I could dwell any longer on the thought, Anne was saying, "I have arranged with Merle Park that the classes take place in her private studio in Hammersmith."

At least I knew, because of the pedigree of this beautiful ballerina, that there would be a sprung floor. Many times in my student years, I had watched in awe through a glass window as Merle Park rehearsed in the company studio with the Royal Ballet.

Anne was now telling me the importance of privacy and that no one should know about the classes. She stressed this point. Further instructions were given:

"You will arrive before Her Royal Highness and be inside the studio waiting for her. She will enter with her detective."

"When speaking she should always be addressed by her title, 'Your Royal Highness.'"

"After the class, if you would wait ten minutes before leaving, please."

Anne then thanked me "for taking this on" and handed me the keys for the studio and a proposed schedule of the dates, along with her telephone number in case there were any conflicts with the scheduled times.

When I had a quick glance at the paper, I chuckled with glee. It was on Buckingham Palace letterhead.

She said that it was a pleasure to meet me and, getting up to leave, gestured for me to stay. Naturally, I said thank you and that I was honoured to take it on.

It was a whirlwind experience, with not a lot of information.

I sat for a minute, sipping my tea from the porcelain cup, enjoying the calmness it brought and the realization that it was, in fact, all real.

CHAPTER THREE

The First Class

THE DATE OF the first class was the following week, which gave me some time to sort myself out.

As ballet mistress of the London City Ballet, I was able to schedule classes and rehearsals for the company and, thankfully, the first class with Princess Diana was early in the morning. This meant I would be able to organize a late morning start for the dancers. I knew they would love that. It would also allow me enough time to get to Chiswick, where the studio was located, and return to Highgate. I had been told by Anne that the early start would not interfere with the Princess's own schedule of royal duties.

I had no idea of what was really required for a class for the Princess.

I knew she had studied ballet when she was young, so at least she would have a basic understanding, but what level had she reached? Anne had mentioned that the Princess liked jazz and modern dance but she had no idea how each style has its own discipline. I chose to prepare various steps and styles that would give me options if we got to that after a warm-up and bit of barre.

I also prepared some choices of music to accompany us, as there would be no pianist.

I had a loose plan in my head, but decided it would be much smarter to remain flexible. Our first meeting would help determine how to proceed. I felt it was much more important that my new student should enjoy herself.

I have always loved working directly with an artist. It allows you the chance to know and understand them, and therefore guide and help them through the work. Of course, this was the Princess of Wales—not quite the same thing.

I now thought of how we should first meet. Would I be in dance clothes, ready to go?

Would that seem weird to her? She would still have to change for class. How would that work?

The whole thing could be hugely embarrassing for both of us. I knew there would be a change room, or at least I thought there would be, so I determined that the Princess could use that and I would scurry to a corner somewhere and do a fast change to be ready before her. Dancers are used to that. Somehow sharing the dressing room didn't seem quite right. I decided it would be much better for our first meeting to be in our regular clothes as two women, before changing into dance clothes and becoming sweaty.

Since this first meeting was very special to me, as it would be something I wanted to remember all my life, I wanted to mark it in my memory. I could think of no better way to do that than to run out to Wallis and buy something new to wear. I've continued doing this throughout my career, and for special family events, receptions, and opening nights. Years later, I heard Hal Prince, the legendary Broadway producer, tell *The Phantom of the Opera* company that the audience should always experience "a sense of the occasion." My meeting with Princess Diana was a few years before *Phantom* hit the stage, but it was indeed a day that would be etched in my mind.

I took the trip to Oxford Circus and made my way to Wallis, one of my favourite stores. Almost immediately, I saw a checkered, black-and-white, rather bold suit.

The skirt was A-line and mid-calf length, the jacket was short to the waist. Wearing a white, red, or black polo neck would be perfect with it. I wouldn't need a coat as, even though it was mid-September. It seemed to call out to me. I bought it, feeling very delighted and trendy. A pair of short black boots, which I had at home, would complete the outfit.

I woke early on first class day, as I wanted to make sure I wasn't late. Emily was just waking up. After morning kisses, she wanted to choose what to wear (a school uniform has its benefits, but that wouldn't start until next year.) She insisted "I can do it by myself" when I tried to help her in an attempt to move things along. Breakfast seemed to take longer than normal and the walk up the hill to school had its usual "Oh look at that, Mummy" stops along the way. Finally, the loving kiss and wave goodbye was achieved. I sprinted back to the apartment, did a fifteen-minute warm-up and stretch and popped into the shower. The water felt wonderful. I took that moment to try to wash off any anxiety I was feeling. My new suit made me feel great and, with my portable cassette tape recorder—remember the 1980s!—and dance bag in hand, I made my way to the subway at Archway. It was a beautiful, crisp September day. I was thankful it wasn't raining.

Getting to Hammersmith went smoothly, as expected. It was the next part of the journey I was concerned about, as I wasn't sure exactly where the studio was. I saw a flower shop as I came out of the station and spontaneously bought a delicate posy of flowers, choosing yellows, the colour of friendship, which I would give to the Princess. I stepped out on to the street and hailed a cab. It occurred to me just then that this was a moment to be enjoyed, and I smiled happily, excited about the meeting.

Once in the taxi, I realized that I should get out before the actual address. I asked the driver to stop at a street nowhere near the street name I had been given. A mild panic came over me, remembering that I had to keep this encounter confidential. I hoped I hadn't made a mistake. The taxi took off and I walked on. It was about half an hour before class and my heart was pounding a little as I picked up my pace to get there.

I had been instructed that there was a private entrance to the studio round the back of the house, and was relieved when I saw it down a laneway. The key turned easily, and I stepped directly into the studio.

It wasn't a huge space but big enough, lovely and bright with barres down the side walls facing the mirrors. A perfect practice room. The thought of Merle Park training here filled me with delight. What an honour to be there and how wonderful of her to allow us into her space. I had been told that no one would be in the house, but I hadn't realized it was part of Merle's home. She was probably rehearsing with the Royal Ballet at the studios on Talgarth Road, which was reasonably close.

I saw two other doors on the other side of the studio and was thrilled to see that they were two dressing rooms. That solved my problem of changing. The slightly bigger room would be good for the Princess. It had wonderful ballet photographs of Merle on the wall, which were inspiring to see.

I set up the cassette tape recorder I had brought and popped in the first cassette so it was ready to go. I took off my boots—one should never wear outdoor shoes on a dance studio floor—and danced round, feeling and enjoying the space. I looked up to see the clock on the wall: in approximately five to ten minutes, Princess Diana would arrive. I slipped my boots back on and waited near the door, holding the flowers.

I heard a car stopping outside and thought it must be her. A few minutes later, the door of the studio opened and in walked the Princess accompanied by two detectives. She walked straight to me, extending her hand and saying, "How lovely to meet you, Anne, and goodness knows what you must think about all this," laughing and blushing profusely. I curtsied and offered her the flowers.

She gave me a warm smile, thanked me, and said how touched she was. I felt she genuinely was. One detective was looking around and checking the rooms and came back to join the other detective, who was a few steps behind us.

"Your Royal Highness," I said, and she instantly replied, "Please call me Diana."

I didn't know what to say so I smiled and kept talking, "I thought you could change in here and then we can start!" At this point, I had no idea whether the detectives were going to stay or leave. If they stayed, it could be awkward. I knew they were probably good at being inconspicuous, but perhaps it wouldn't be so easy in an empty dance studio. Just as I was thinking this, they walked out of the studio, telling us both they would be just outside if we needed anything. *Thank goodness*, I thought.

I showed Diana into the dressing room and then slipped into the other room to quickly change into my dance clothes. I was gently stretching by the barre when she emerged in her black leotard, pink tights, and ballet shoes, her head down. She was obviously uncomfortable. "Please come and stand by the barre and we can chat a little before we start," I said. Her beautiful face was bright red with embarrassment, but she courageously moved towards me.

"Anne, I really don't know what you must think about all this," she repeated.

I simply said, "I love dance and I know you do, too, and that's what we will do here together."

A sigh of relief crossed her face. She lifted her beautiful blue eyes and smiled at me. I was struck by the warmth, sincerity, and intensity of her eyes. The conversation became more fluid as she talked about her early training in ballet, saying she had a tiny bit of tap as well, but that she loved all types of dance. She had not really done any jazz, but thought it looked exciting and could be less demanding than ballet, which she felt she might be too tall for and not terribly good at.

"Watching ballet, I am in awe of the dancers, I absolutely love it," she said.

I suggested we do different styles, but first we must always start with a good warm-up.

During the warm-up, I would be able to determine what we could tackle.

I asked her to face me with one hand on the barre, and we would start with our feet parallel, arms in second position. I wanted her to feel she had something to hold onto for support and by facing me she would be able to follow my steps. As she placed her left hand on the barre, I caught a glimpse of her dazzling blue sapphire ring.

Her head continued to look at the floor. I gently noted that the head was the heaviest part of the body, suggesting that if she placed her hand on her heart, there would be a natural reaction where the heart would open and lift, opening the shoulders, and the chin and head would follow, making it easier. Her discomfort still evident, she tried it. I put the music on, and she began to relax. Music is such an important aspect of dance, whether for class or on stage. Ballet class music tends to be more regimented, with repetitive rhythms designed for accuracy as you repeat the movement, but I had chosen something that was rhythmic, yet had a fun melody and was contemporary in feel.

I took her through some basic jazz barre exercises. She followed along nicely as we warmed up with parallel demi pliés, relaxing the knee and ankle joints. Next, to warm up her back, I showed her how to roll gently through the spine, bending forward and recovering, then pulling on the barre by lifting her outside arm with a balletic port de bras to complete a few side stretches. Following that were gentle back bends, or cambré in ballet terms, always returning to our centre and stopping for a minute to hold our pose so we could work on lifting our heads.

Diana had beautiful long legs and arms. I could see the potential of her line as she moved them, but, more importantly, I could see how she enjoyed it. We moved to the centre of the studio floor and I taught a gentle jazz combination that was free and moving. This cemented for me her passion for movement. I wanted her to feel the freedom that dance can give, and she did.

Diana responded beautifully, losing her inhibitions to just enjoy herself. We only took breaks when I changed music, and we repeated each combo several times. I then went to some tiny jumps in first and second position to get her cardio going and took some moving steps across the room.

I noticed we were over the hour, the time had flown by, and suggested we finish by just stretching out on the floor to relax for a few minutes.

One of the detectives popped his head in to acknowledge that time was up. The Princess thanked him as she lay there.

After a few minutes, she thanked me and told me how much she had enjoyed the class and looked forward to next week. She went into the dressing room to change back into her clothes. I decided to quietly wait till she came out. I collected the tape recorder and cassettes.

The detective was outside the door. Diana, having changed and holding the posy of flowers, gave a gentle knock on it, and turned to me to thank me again. I curtsied to her. The detective quickly opened the door and she was whisked away.

I felt relieved, but also very happy that the class had gone well. I felt that it had been a very special meeting.

CHAPTER FOUR

And 5, 6, 7, 8 Continues

THE IDEA OF keeping the class my personal secret brought a smile to my face as I travelled to Highgate, having waited the requested ten minutes before leaving the studio. And even though I felt a bit silly doing so, I checked carefully as I opened the door to make sure no one was around. The coast was clear. I walked for a bit, enjoying the wonderful experience I had just had. By luck, I discovered a bus route that took me to the tube station. I was back at the ballet studio in time to rehearse with the company, still in a state of euphoria that all had gone well.

My little darling was in a playful mood when I picked her up after my rehearsal, and we played all the way home. Walking through the park, we stopped to see the swans on the pond, as always. Seeing the joy in a young one's eyes is glorious. I was reminded of the brilliance of the choreography for *Swan Lake* as I watched the swans glide over the water.

After dinner we followed our nighttime ritual of chatting about the day and what we were going to do tomorrow, read two books, and said goodnight to the tree outside, along with anyone else we could think of, before she was ready for sleep. With any excuse to stay awake, Emily asked when she was going to see the dancing again. I promised Saturday, if she went to sleep. Complete bribery, but sometimes it's necessary, as most mums understand. Emily, to watch rehearsals for a little while, would sit with Daddy, who was the lighting designer for the company, enthralled by the dancers. When they were on their break, they would fuss over her—she loved that, too!

We rehearsed in Highgate United Reformed Church, at the corner of Hornsey Lane and Cromwell Avenue: an unusual choice for a ballet company, but it made a wonderful home for the London City Ballet, which was still very much a start-up company. The original Presbyterian church dates back to 1887 and had been very popular in its day, but it had to merge with the Highgate Congregational Church on Pond Square to become the Highgate United Reform Church in order to keep going. Worship had been diminished to one day a week, Sunday, which was usually the dancers' day off. We practised in the main community room and were able to rent other areas of the church for storing set pieces, costumes, and props. The church caretakers were grateful, as it kept the church financially afloat, for a little while at least. In 1982, this wonderful neo-Gothic church was converted into apartment units, fortunately keeping its magnificent façade. At the time, our flat was directly across the road, on Cromwell Avenue, which was perfect and a time saver.

The following week, my class with the Princess was on Wednesday. There was always a little bit of me that couldn't quite believe that I was meeting Diana, but, at the same time, it gave me a constant inner smile. I wondered how she would feel after having her first class.

That Wednesday, I began what would become my routine. I took the tube to Chiswick, this time managing to get a bus instead of a taxi after the subway. It dropped me close to Merle Park's studio, necessitating a short walk. I arrived fifteen to twenty minutes prior to the Princess, giving me enough time to set up music, change into dance clothes, and do a bit of a warm-up.

I heard the car arriving, and a few minutes later the Princess stepped into the studio with a big smile, saying, "It's me again," still blushing apologetically. I told her I was so happy to see her and asked how her body felt after last week. "I felt wonderful, but my body was a bit stiff the next morning. I didn't know you could have aches in so many places," she laughed.

I remember thinking how beautifully open and honest she was, with the most infectious giggle. "I'll just pop in to change, Anne." It was helpful to hear how she was so as I could work out the best way to continue the class.

As a teacher you must be able to balance how much to push a student while always ensuring that the technique of using the muscles correctly is in place. This was not a regular student studying dance for a career, but someone whose job was to go on to a full day of engagements, often well into the evening, although at this point, it wasn't long after the honeymoon. Full schedules and her diary were still being created, she said. "I just want to do a good job," she told me later that day. "Whatever that job is, being the Princess of Wales!"

Coming out of the change room, she walked over to the barre, her head looking down towards the floor and her face flushed pink. She was wearing the same three-quarter sleeve black leotard and pink ballet tights with her ballet shoes, as before. I had noticed during the first class that her underwear was showing below her leotard and tights—what looked like Marks and Spencer knickers were very evident. This made me giggle inside. I thought that at the right time I would suggest a dancer's trick of what to wear below tights. I didn't think that would be today, as she was suffering enough shyness and embarrassment by just standing before me. It crossed my mind that Diana probably had led a relatively sheltered life until now. She was obviously body conscious. In fairness to her, wearing dance gear can leave anyone feeling exposed and vulnerable.

We started into the class and I repeated the same warm-up that we did the previous week. This would slowly allow the Princess to know what was coming and be prepared so as we could improve every time. The main thing I wanted to work on was lifting her head and gently opening her shoulders. It would help her to stand confidently.

In classical ballet, we use the word *repetiteur* to indicate repeat, and, in rehearsal, we repeat and repeat to perfect the movement. That movement then becomes one with us. It is only then that we can transform each movement into dance without thinking. Being in that very moment gives us the freedom to express our interpretation of the dance.

As we went through the same barre routine, warming every part of the body in both ballet and jazz form, she began to relax. Dancers work at the barre to centre and balance the body, working each side equally. In fact, the origin of the ballet dancer's hair worn in a bun and divided in the centre by a part was to ensure that each side of the body at the barre was used the same way and perfected on each side before stepping into the centre of the room. This is designed to secure perfection of balance when both sides have been worked equally. Often one side of our body feels better than the other, and barre exercises are designed to eradicate that feeling.

With her long arms, I wanted to find a way for Diana to use the full extension of them. I explained that if the movement for her upper body was coming from her back and then continuing through to her arms, this would help her carry her head in a straight line.

This was something I had learned from the renowned Royal Ballet prima ballerina Svetlana Beriosova when she coached me through the

Lilac Fairy variation from *The Sleeping Beauty*. Full of serenity and grace when she was a dancer, I was in awe when I worked with her. Svetlana understood my fear in tackling such a demanding virtuosic variation, requiring both a strong technique and a royal command—the Lilac Fairy is the Queen of the Fairies. The character had to trust her inner power and bestow wisdom on others. The upper body best expresses that, she told me, by holding the head with pride of authority.

I told the Princess the story of how Svetlana gave me the confidence and help I needed by trusting myself. She listened, enthralled. She told me again how she absolutely loved ballet and wished she could have been a ballet dancer, but felt she was too tall and probably didn't have the discipline that was required. I could see in her face how much she did love the art and that she longed to know more and hear more about what dancers go through to attain their goals.

Coming into the centre, I chose to do a very lyrical combination using arms reaching high and low, with lots of breadth of movement, so she could enjoy the freedom. I wanted her to feel the energy right to the end of her fingers and, hopefully, that place beyond. I could see the magical look on her face as she experienced this new extension of herself. I then moved to some jazz hip exercises for a change of theme, creating a flowing and fun routine.

For this routine, I used the 5, 6, 7, 8 count, which Diana was delighted to hear, joining in with me as we practised the movements a few times. She was in her element! We both got a good sweat going, then relaxed on the floor, lying flat as we did some deep breathing and relaxation to calm the muscles.

And then the hour was up. Diana thanked me profusely, kissing me on both cheeks as she said her goodbyes. She was then ushered to her car, which sped off, back to the palace.

I have had the best laugh watching the episode of *The Crown* where Diana is portrayed taking a dancing class. Why was the casting of the ballet teacher so stereotypical of what is presumed to be a firm, ungiving ballet teacher? If only people knew what had been going on in our private sessions.

Our classes continued in this way over the next few weeks, with me adding more advanced levels of intensity into our routines while keeping them fun. I also added in some tap dancing every few lessons, which was a wonderful way of using a different style and creating intricate rhythms, as well as being an excellent cardio workout.

It was now coming to the end of October and we were both more comfortable with each other. Our conversations became very easy. The Princess was going on her first official tour: "with Charles to Wales," she told me.

I asked if she was excited. She confided that she was a little nervous. That first performance always gives one butterflies, I said, and assured her she would be wonderful! She laughed and said, "Oh, I hope so!"

On her return, I congratulated the Princess on her first official royal visit, and she said she was completely overwhelmed by the warmth she felt from the people. How kind everyone had been. "I think my speech in Welsh was a disaster, and I've never shaken as many hands before, I will have to get better at all that," she said. This cemented for me that she had a strong sense of duty and was going to take her role very seriously.

At the end of the class, she asked if she could have five minutes to chat. Of course, I said. I wondered whether maybe she did not want to continue with her classes and was fully prepared for that. I had quietly told myself that I would enjoy our time together for as long as it lasted and that it was an honour to share my love of dance with her.

"Anne, I wanted to tell you that a little one is on the way. I'm pregnant!"

I spontaneously threw my arms around her in congratulations. Maybe not appropriate, but an instinctive action on my part, as it is for many women. She beamed back at me, and we shared a joyous moment, just two ladies together. I immediately thought of the class we had just done and took a gulp, as it had been quite demanding. She continued speaking: "I wanted to let you know that, once the announcement is made, 'they' will not let me take classes anymore, but I would like to keep it going for as long as I can, and I don't want to be fussed over. After all, lots of ladies have babies."

"Of course," I said admiring her guts, "but we must stop the minute you need to." She assured me that she did not want to stop, but because the baby would be the "heir to the throne," she supposed they would want her to be careful.

I asked if her husband was delighted, and she said, "Yes, Charles is thrilled." She was glowing as she told me, the start of motherhood shining through.

"'Baby Wales' will be with me in class, and I promise I will not overdo it," she said.

We were able to achieve just one more class before the announcement of her pregnancy came from Buckingham Palace, on November 5, 1981, a little over three months after the fairy tale wedding. The wonderful news was received with great excitement from the public.

At our last class, we had said a warm goodbye to each other. She shared with me that she had less energy and had started having morning sickness. We commiserated at how hard that can be as you go from horizontal to vertical when getting out of bed. I knew the feeling well.

"Once baby is born, can we please resume our classes, Anne, of course, depending on how your schedule is? It will be a wonderful way to get back into shape and I do love the chance to get away from everything for an hour."

I was naturally thrilled at the prospect, but in truth wasn't sure that the classes would continue the next year mainly because of the Princess's duties and the demands that a new little precious one would bring.

CHAPTER FIVE

Baby Wales One

THE TRADITIONAL ANNOUNCEMENT of the birth of the Princess of Wales's son was declared in writing and read aloud at the gates of Buckingham Palace on June 21, 1982, as an enthusiastic crowd enthusiastically looked on. Cheers rang out when the news was heard.

The notice read "Her Royal Highness the Princess of Wales was safely delivered of a son at 9:03 p.m. today. Her Royal Highness and her child are both doing well." The name of the future king would not be announced until a week later: His Royal Highness Prince William Arthur Philip Louis of Wales.

I was thrilled for Diana that it was a boy and, as she told me later, she had done her duty and produced an heir. I knew she would be ecstatic and adore this precious bundle which we, the public, had the delight of peeking at when she left St. Mary's Hospital with Charles the next day. How brave I thought she was, coming down the steps of the hospital once Charles had passed their son back to her. I could see the usual flush of embarrassment on her face and her head shyly tilted to the side, and thought how utterly exhausted she must be. But she smiled and held her little one close to her as she gracefully got into the waiting car.

I was particularly thrilled as my own daughter, Emily, was having her fifth birthday party that day. How extraordinary that they should share the same birth date on summer solstice, the beginning of summer.

A new opportunity had arisen for me that summer. I had just left London City Ballet and was now ballet mistress for Wayne Sleep. I greatly admired the ex-Royal Ballet dancer, who was forming a new company for his innovative show *Dash*.

I loved Wayne's work and had seen him perform in Andrew Lloyd Webber's musical *Song & Dance* earlier that year, as well as in the role of Mr. Mistoffelees in *Cats*, which he created, working closely with the choreographer Gillian Lynne.

Wayne was practising at Pineapple Dance Studios, and I had just finished a class myself when I decided I would go and speak with him. We instantly hit it off, so, when I mentioned that I had heard he might be looking for some help with his company, I was offered the job. I was thrilled. I had always been excited by the potential of every aspect of dance, not just ballet, and this would allow me to experience new choreography in different styles, as well as learn how to build a show.

I was so thankful to Wayne for giving me the opportunity. He didn't really know me, but because of my Royal Ballet background and the fact that I was Scottish (his manager George Lawson, whom he trusted implicitly, was also Scottish), he took a chance.

It was hard to leave London City Ballet, but I was very excited at the scope of working with Wayne. I left the ballet sure in the knowledge that I would always be invited back, which made me very happy, and I remained close to everyone at the company, visiting them often.

It was late August of that year when I got the call from Diana's lady-in-waiting, Anne Beckwith-Smith, who asked me how my diary was for the next while as the Princess would like to do some dancing. I was flabbergasted. I really hadn't thought the classes would resume. By September, Diana and I were back in the studio.

I was excited to see the Princess again and anxious to hear how she was and if she was loving being a mum. She greeted me with such warmth, and for most of the lesson we talked about babies. She seemed tired, which is natural in the first few months after childbirth, even if you have help from a nanny or family. Sleep deprivation and constant worrying all come into play for a first-time mum. Diana told me she absolutely adored her son and wanted to spend all her time with him, that she couldn't sleep because she wanted to keep checking on him. All very natural emotions.

We did a very gentle class that day, focusing on centring and carefully strengthening her core. Afterwards she said she felt much more energized. I was delighted.

At our next class, we had just heard the devastating news about the death of Princess Grace of Monaco. I could see how upsetting this was for Diana. She said Grace had been very kind and caring to her. She wanted to go to the funeral, but had been told by her husband that it wasn't appropriate to do so. She could not understand why and did not want to go against her husband's wishes, but felt very strongly about it. She decided she would go to the boss, the Queen, to ask permission, which the Queen granted, seeing no reason why Diana should not be the royal family's representative. It meant a great deal to Diana to pay her personal respects, as well as that of the family, as she put it.

Our classes continued on almost a weekly basis, and I could start to see a difference in Diana's line and strength. We shared a lot of laughter and had fun. She loved the fact we were hidden away in a studio without anyone knowing. Music was her other huge love and you could see and feel the joy it gave her when she was dancing. We would use many different contemporary artists for the jazz part of our classes. She loved Billy Joel and Duran Duran. Coincidentally, I was to assist Arlene Phillips on the video for Duran Duran's "The Wild Boys" a couple of years later. And Billy Joel's "Uptown Girl" would be Diana's choice for her secret performance at Covent Garden, but that also was still in the future.

That fall, it was announced that the Prince and Princess would make their first official overseas visit, a tour of Australia, in March 1983. The lead-up to it was fraught. Diana expressed her concerns to me. "I do not want to be away from my son for six weeks; that is just far too long at his age. I just don't want to be a mother that's not around, even though I understand that my duties might take me away from time to time; this is just too long." I totally understood how she felt. I could not even imagine it for myself, and especially at such a milestone in a child's life where you don't want to miss the first time your little one stands and takes their first steps by themselves. You just want to be close to them and give them love.

It was a huge dilemma for Diana, but when she talked about it, her voice was always gentle as she thoughtfully worked through deciding what she could do. It continued to weigh on her. Royal children had always been left at home so as not to interfere with their routine when their parents travelled. If Diana took her son to Australia, she would be going against the norm and she didn't want to cause "a fuss." She had been told that it was very important, politically, to make a good impression in Australia, and naturally she wanted to do a good job for her husband and the Queen.

As the weeks passed, her schedule was busy with preparations of both her diary and her wardrobe. She was tired, and still a decision had not been made about Baby William. I could see the pressure she was under.

"I've considered all the points, Anne, and although it will be challenging, I believe that I can take William with me if the schedule is well organized, and I am going to tell them." I was immensely proud of her, as I knew how hard it had been to arrive at this decision. There was also a sense of relief for her in starting to assert herself. She was still only twenty-one years old.

Throughout the tour, I watched television avidly in hopes of seeing images of her and to see how things were going. The footage was wonderful, particularly when she was holding William and when she and Charles were together, often holding hands. The crowds were unbelievable. People seemed to come from everywhere to get a glimpse of her. She was so natural when she was near any children, crouching down to have a moment with them, and she looked beautifully elegant at every event. The highlight for me was when she and Charles danced at a formal function held in their honour. She was wearing a stunning blue gown. He moved very well and confidently with his wife, but was continually spinning her round in an awkward manner. It must have left her quite dizzy. You could see the glow on her face, however, and they looked tremendously happy. Everyone adored seeing the royal couple in this way.

On her return, I told her how amazing she was and what a success the tour had been. "Oh, Anne, do you really think so?" she responded. "Nobody has said a word about it since I've been back." I was aghast and reiterated my words. "I'm so thankful you think that," she said. "I wasn't at all sure. It was tremendously hot and stuffy some days and with so many people it felt a bit overwhelming. I was given so many flowers and asked so many times how William was," she said with a giggle. "They called my name a lot and I wanted to make sure that I said hello to as many people as possible as they had come out to see us."

I told her how very special it was to see her dancing with Charles, and she said, "I hope you thought I looked okay."

"Wonderful," I assured her.

It was then she confided in me that she was a little worried about the attention she got as it seemed to bother Charles a bit. "I do love him so and want to make him happy and to be proud of me as his wife."

I could sense there was such vulnerability there and realized how difficult it must be if there is no one to give you support or tell you that you are doing a good job. Part of the delight after an important event is to share it with family and friends.

By her return, *Dash* had opened at the Apollo Victoria Theatre in London and I had been lucky that, while the Princess was in Australia, I had been able to rehearse with Wayne and the *Dash* company leading up to the opening. The Princess was interested in the show and its concept and had seen Wayne when he was dancing with the Royal Ballet. She was a big fan. The word "dash" is defined in the dictionary as "to knock, throw, hurtle, or thrust," and anyone who has seen Wayne knows his fast-darting energy and brilliant technique. He had wanted to create a revue-type show that made dance accessible, appealing, and enjoyable for the audience.

At one of our classes a few weeks later, Diana asked me if she could go to see the show, but she did not want it to be like an official visit—could she just go backstage? My immediate thought was, *It's a bit crazy in the wings of any show, and this one is very fast-paced, would she be safe?* I did know that coming on and off the set wasn't too problematic, but there was always a danger element if you were not experienced in how things worked, not to mention a nightmare for security as that part of the stage would be pitch black.

I explained that I would have to ask Wayne and that he didn't know that I was giving her private sessions. I had at this point only told my husband, as it was getting difficult to explain where I was going every week. I had also told my darling Scottish mum, who just said, "Lovely, dear, and don't forget we all pee the same way!" She was, though a big supporter of the royal family.

The Princess said, "Let's ask Wayne. I'd love to meet him." I then warned the Princess that Wayne had created a very amusing skit based on her son, William, and wore a babygrow. She burst out laughing and said that she had to see it.

Wayne, naturally, was thrilled at the idea of Diana coming backstage and promised to be discreet about the plan. We thought it best that she come for the second half of the show, since the full show was very long. If she sat through it all, there would be an unnecessary risk of people seeing her at the intermission and the press could get wind of her being there. This way we would sneak her out quickly at the end of the show before the last bows were taken.

The plan was that I was to be at the stage door to meet her at the assigned time and slip her and her detectives into the theatre, then take them to the left corner of the backstage area a few minutes before the curtain went up on the second act. With stage management's help, we had left a seat for her there. It was also the safest place for her to sit, as there were not as many entrances and exits in that area. I was in fear of anything going wrong, but also excited at the possibility of hopefully getting away with it.

My heart was pounding as Diana arrived and we went backstage, the stage doorman nodding nicely to us as we entered. One of the detectives stayed at the door while the other accompanied us into the theatre. We met Wayne at the designated spot a few minutes before his entrance and there was an instant rapport between them. Diana loved the whole atmosphere backstage and Wayne was a rascal, occasionally playing to the corner where she was sitting, rather than out front, which made her grin from ear to ear. None of the other company members were aware of her presence until they saw her as they were preparing to make entrances. When they did realize it was Diana watching in the wings, well, it made for an electric Act 2. The Baby Wales number was a favourite for Diana, and Wayne remarked to me how much he loved that she could laugh at herself and accept the intended humour.

During the applause at the end of the show, the detective came back to her side and we exited quickly, leaving through the stage door. She went straight into the car that was waiting for her and was gone. We had done it. The press never knew.

CHAPTER SIX

Facing Difficult Realities
of Ballet Life

S HORTLY AFTER OUR night-out adventure, we met for another
class and were resting on the floor after our routines.

By this time, Diana had graduated from traditional black
leotard, pink tights, and leather ballet shoes to more comfortable unitards
in different colours or matching tights and leotards with white jazz shoes,
which were more suitable to the movements we did. They made how she
moved so much easier. She had given me a pale-yellow dance outfit as a
thank-you present after I had suggested she wear a G-string as underwear.
"It works so much better," she said, laughing loudly.

Looking back at the style for dance in the 1980s is very funny. We
looked ridiculous, but we didn't go as far as Jane Fonda with her matching
headbands.

Diana asked me about my time as ballet mistress with the London
City Ballet. I said how much I had loved it. She was interested in knowing
the background to the company. I explained that I felt it was incredibly

brave of Harold with his then-wife, Marian St. Claire, and dance partner, Michael Beare, to want to create the London City Ballet as a bold new independent company. The challenges were huge, especially if there was no Arts Council funding.

Harold, Marian, Michael, and I had all been members in the early days of the Scottish Ballet, under the artistic direction of Peter Darrell, and our careers had taken us in different directions. Mine took me to a brand-new company called Ballet International under Larry Long and Ben Stevenson, as I wanted to experience American choreographers and travel, which we did, to South Africa. During that trip, I experienced an incident that is indelible in my mind and that I must mention because it brought me face to face with racism and the harsh reality of discrimination.

I was so shamefully ignorant at that point in my life. It was September 1976 and the Ballet International was performing in Johannesburg. It had never occurred to me that we would have to dance in front of a segregated audience. I was horrified. I lacked any understanding of the politics of the country. The shock hit me and my fellow dancers like a thunderbolt. We were under contract, and the segregation had not been brought to the dancers' attention by management, whether by an innocent decision or by choice, or through the presumption that we were all aware of the reality of apartheid. We were told we had to perform. It made me realize what a sheltered life I had lived, a white ballet dancer from a privileged country. The expression "bun-head ballet dancer" seemed to ring true. My eyes had been opened. The result was me making a pledge to myself to always be aware of racism and to always fight against it. On our return to London, we made other dancers aware of the abhorrent experience. The company ran into financial difficulties shortly after that tour and had to be dissolved.

Although it was now many years since the Scottish Ballet, Harold, Marian, Michael, and I had all danced together over the years and I had always kept in touch with them. I was delighted when, in 1980, I received a phone call from Harold. He wanted to invite me to join his new venture, a brand-new ballet company called the London City Ballet.

At first, the London City Ballet was quite small, performing only lunch-hour performances at the Arts Theatre Club in Leicester Square. A new concept for ballet. The company was received very well. Harold wished to expand performances and tour the smaller theatres in the U.K. to reach varied audiences that could not afford the expense of Covent Garden. He asked me to join the company as both a dancer and as ballet mistress. The timing could not have been better for me.

Michael was the ballet master, who also performed principal roles and partnered with Marian, who was fondly nicknamed Midge. Midge and Michael danced beautifully together; theirs was a dream partnership, each of them offering outstanding technique that embodied elegance, grace, and passion. Rehearsing with them was a joy. They were self-disciplined and open to suggestions about their work, always accepting feedback no matter how small, and open to incorporating changes into their work. Their mantra, like that of so many accomplished artists, was to bring excellence to any stage on which they were performing.

The program Harold wanted to create had to appeal to both balletomane and newcomer alike. Very often, the stages were not conducive for dance, sometimes not having a sprung floor, which was not good for the dancers' muscles; however, the energy and willingness of this young, happy, vibrant company was palpable, and if it meant reaching more of an audience, we would do it.

Harold was a whiz at finding private financial backing to keep the company afloat, but he knew that getting the right recognition would be the only way to keep the London City Ballet sustainable. As it turned out, he had written to the Princess of Wales, inviting her to become the patron of the company. This is what she told me that morning. She wanted to know what I thought about it. She told me that she had a few charities that had been suggested to her when she first became Charles's wife. "I care very much about each one of them," she explained, "especially the cancer fund for children, it breaks my heart when I see the effects of cancer on a child. Also, the Royal School for the Blind, as I can't begin to imagine what that must be like not to be able see so many beautiful things in the world. This request from Harold King would be something which is very dear to my heart and that is my love for ballet. Princess Margaret is patron of the London Festival Ballet so they can't really ask her, although I know she is a huge ballet lover, too, and the Royal Ballet, of course, belongs to the Queen. If I can't be a ballet dancer, I like the idea of being able to help this new company as they desperately need it."

A special informal visit had been planned so she could see the company rehearsing. Diana loved experiencing the atmosphere of the rehearsal and especially enjoyed being able to talk to the dancers. As for the dancers, they thought it was thrilling as she was so genuinely interested in them and their lives. The Princess became patron, and she would return for several visits to watch the company.

During her visits, Diana had become very interested in one specific dancer. This dancer was of a very slim physique, with a good technique and an angelic look, all perfect traits for a ballet dancer. I had worked with her when I was ballet mistress of the company and knew her well. Having seen this dancer on a few occasions, the Princess noticed that she seemed to be very hard on herself when she landed badly from a triple pirouette. Diana also mentioned to me that the dancer was looking much thinner on one of her subsequent visits. I was extremely worried when she told me this, as this dancer had a history of bulimia.

In fact, I have seen bulimia too often in young dancers who pursue what they see to be physical perfection. It is a very serious mental and physical condition.

My eyes had first been opened to the disease when I was training at the Royal Ballet School. I used to spend a lot of time in the small rehearsal room on Talgarth Road where the Royal Ballet School studios were located, and was usually joined by two beautiful dancers who were in a different class and a year ahead. Naturally, I was in awe of them.

When I came into the rehearsal room one day, they were both discussing how they could get around the next day's weigh-in. I really had no idea what they were talking about and carried on while I listened. I was only eighteen, and a little naive. They both decided that they would weigh enough to be able to take class if they would put tiny weights in the lining of their leotards when they stepped on the weight. They had been warned that if they lost any more pounds, they would not be allowed to dance. They thought they would fool the teachers and medics. Their plan did not work, and they were stopped from doing any further classes until such time as they reached a suitable weight, and then they would be watched diligently to see that it was maintained. There was particular interest in them, as they both had outstanding technique and "Madame" Ninette De Valois, the founder of the Royal Ballet, had recognized their work. This, of course, was huge.

I didn't see them for the next few weeks. They did return to school, but much later I found out that they had been allowed back on condition that they received the supervised help they needed to conquer this difficult disease. In later years, one of the dancers went on to become a principal with a South African ballet company.

Her story ended well, unlike that of a dear classmate and friend of mine whose name happened to be Diane. She was a beautiful dancer and extremely shy, and we had gravitated to each other the first week of school. Neither of us were sure whether we would fit in amidst the confident dancers who had very affluent parents and had come up through White Lodge, the early training school for the Royal Ballet. I was on scholarship, so I felt a very big responsibility to do well, and Diane thought that they had made a mistake in her case—that she was not good enough to be there at all. We supported each other through our different fears.

We would both go to Freed's at Leicester Square to pick up our ballet shoes. Most students would order ten pairs at a time, but Diane and I could only afford four at a time and had to make them last. We treasured the beautiful pink satin shoes that were made to fit our feet. It was a very special event. We would take ourselves for a treat afterwards. This usually meant a coffee shop and cake. I began to notice that Diane was not ordering cake as she used to and usually only had an herbal tea. At first, I thought maybe she did not want to spend the money, as we were on tight budgets, but she would just say she wasn't hungry. By the end of that first year of school, she had lost a tremendous amount of weight and was looking weak in class. She was sent home, never to return.

It was some months later that I received a letter from her saying how sorry she was. She was suffering from anorexia nervosa, but was now slowly starting to heal and that she would not be returning to school. I was heartbroken.

How could I not see this, and what would I have done if I had? It is very difficult to recognize symptoms and sometimes you only see them when it's too late, but these incidents certainly made me so much more aware.

I had a scary incident myself in my early ballet career, a few years after ballet school. I was in Canada and attending classes with Lois Smith, the most exquisite dancer and Canada's initial prima ballerina. She was an outstanding woman and a brilliant teacher, from whom I learned a great deal. She was kind to me and organized an audition for Les Grands Ballets Canadiens, as she thought my style would best suit that company. I was thrilled at the opportunity and went to do classes with them in Montreal.

Linda Stearns was the ballet mistress. After a few days of classes, she invited me to her office to chat. She said that she liked my work, and that they might need extra dancers for their Christmas season of *The Nutcracker*, but to get the contract I would have to lose ten pounds. The contract would be dependent on auditioning in six weeks' time, when I would have to show I had lost the weight.

I knew I had put on a little bit of weight since I left the Scottish Ballet on a year's sabbatical, but did not think it was that much. I was excited at the opportunity of dancing with a Canadian company and determined to make it work, so I went on what I thought was a strict but healthy diet. I returned to Montreal at the designated time to audition.

As I was getting ready for class and doing my hair in the mirror of the dressing room, I looked across to see who the person was being reflected in the opposite mirror, as she was someone I did not recognize. I turned round to see myself! I was truly shocked. I had not realized how much weight I had lost. This realization made me acutely aware of dieting's potential dangers for young dancers and, although I got the job, I would never diet again.

All these different experiences taught me to be more perceptive to the challenges that ballet dancers face. I shared my stories with Princess Diana when she mentioned this dancer at the London City Ballet. I also explained to Diana why I was concerned on hearing her astute observation. It was during my time as ballet mistress with the London City Ballet, just over a year before, when I first suspected the same dancer whom Diana had mentioned had an eating disorder.

In my role as ballet mistress, I watched keenly over every aspect of the dancers' lives. I had noticed how much weight this dancer was losing, as well as how hard it was for her to finish class. Her body seemed to lack strength that had been previously present. She would often stop halfway through an exercise out of sheer frustration. I could also see that the other dancers were aware, too, as her vitality and mood had become very different. Since I suspected that she was suffering from bulimia, I knew I had to approach her thoughtfully to carefully help her understand how serious this could be for her health and to assist her in getting the help she needed.

When approached, she was in complete denial, bursting into tears and adamantly saying this was not the case. I expressed that I wanted to help and asked if she would see someone, just to talk. I had to be firm as I was sure that my instinct was right and that she would try everything not to face it. I ultimately had to tell her I would speak to her parents and that she would not be allowed to perform until then. Crying and protesting vehemently at the thought of losing performances, she agreed.

She was hospitalized for three months and given the psychiatric help she needed, and was able to return to the company six months later. Since this can be a recurring disease, with the information that I had received from Diana, I would now check in with the company to make sure that she was in no danger. I knew the company would keep a rigid eye on her and advise her.

Diana listened intently, not commenting, and appeared to be shocked.

CHAPTER SEVEN

Baby Wales Two

DIANA CONTINUED TO visit the company regularly after becoming patron of the London City Ballet, showing support whenever she could. The attention she gave was instrumental in garnering the international reputation the company deserved.

The ballet was scheduled to premiere a new production of *Carmen* in Oslo, Norway, at the Konserthus on February 11, 1984. This was exciting for the company and for the Princess, as she had watched many rehearsals and couldn't wait to see the final production on stage with set and costume. She cared so deeply about its success that she had agreed to attend the event, making it an official solo visit. Diana enthusiastically told me she had chosen a red dress with a lace top, as she felt this would suit the mood of the ballet. I was no longer the ballet mistress for the company, although I had the privilege of being allowed to drop in to see rehearsals, but would not be in attendance at the performance in Oslo.

Diana and I met for class shortly before the premiere and had a lot of fun working through some basic flamenco moves. I'm not sure that we correctly honoured the dance's history, but we certainly enjoyed portraying its style, intensity, and rhythms. We ended up laughing on the floor.

Then to my amazement, with a beaming smile, Diana told me she was pregnant and that the baby was due in September, but they wouldn't announce it to the world until after she came back from Norway. "If I get away with it! You know what the press are like, always looking for an exclusive."

I could not have been happier for her. I could see she was filled with joy and was having a little devilish fun. "Anne, it's so upsetting because I will probably have to stop classes again. The press will be watching my every move and there is always a concern that everything goes all right with the pregnancy, but I hope we can start again after the baby is born, and you must *come to tea.*"

At that time, I had no idea what "coming to tea" meant, but I would soon discover its meaning. I told her I would love to come to tea and to continue the classes, but only if it was possible for her. I understood if she couldn't continue should her schedule of being "a mum of two" and the Princess of Wales become too much. We had a warm hug before saying goodbye.

Her solo visit to Norway on February 11 went well and she did get away with it: that is, keeping her pregnancy out of the news until her return to London. The palace made the formal announcement on Valentine's Day, February 14, 1984, much to the delight of the public who saw this announcement as the continuing love story of Charles and Diana. The Princess certainly glowed. I wrote to congratulate her on "getting away with it" and received a letter back from her in which she acknowledged her success:

> *I never imagined that we'd actually announce it before the press.*
> *I spent the entire time, breathing in just in case someone saw a tiny bump. . . .*
> *Now, everyone I meet shakes my hand, looking at my stomach!*

The timing of our break during Diana's second pregnancy couldn't have worked better for me, as Wayne was heading into a second season of *The Hot Shoe Show*, which had been very successful the previous year. The Princess loved watching it on television and delighted hearing about the process. I was thrilled to be a part of the second season, where I would again take all the rehearsals and be the eyes for Wayne during the filming. The show was wonderfully innovative for its time and showed huge initiative on the part of the BBC to take a risk with a variety dance show. Each dancer was chosen for their specific style and uniqueness. They included Bonnie Langford, who is now a television and West End favourite (London's West End is the equivalent to Broadway in New York); Cherry Gillespie, an original member of Pan's People, an all-female dance group who performed regularly on the famous hit show *Top of the Pops*; Finola Hughes, who originated the role of Victoria, the White Cat in *Cats*, went on to star in the film *Staying Alive* with John Travolta, and is now best known for starring in *General Hospital*; Jane Darling, who was the most spectacular jazz dancer; Linda Mae Brewer, who was an outstanding tap dancer; and Claud Paul Henry and Stewart Avon Arnold, who were brilliant contemporary dancers. There were also many guests throughout the season who would join us for an episode.

For me, the highlight was being able to work with the choreographers, including Anthony Van Laast, who would much later choreograph the hit shows *Mama Mia!*, *Joseph and the Amazing Technicolor Dreamcoat*, and *Sister Act*; Arlene Phillips from *Starlight Express* and *We Will Rock You*; Christopher Bruce, renowned choreographer of the London Contemporary Dance Theatre; and, of course, Wayne, who always pushed everything to the height of excellence. He understood the possibility of dance for television— all the dynamic visuals—and while there had been difficulties in the first year, he saw opportunity to improve. He had a very keen eye for design both in set and costume and often his creative idea for a number would inform that, using special effects to heighten the performance. Numbers like "Flight of the Bumble Bee," where Wayne danced the role of the bee annoying Julian Webber as he played the cello, and "Pinball Wizard," in which he represented the ball of the pinball machine, certainly lived up to the title of the show. Those feet were hot!

I was there to run rehearsals and to ensure that if another take was needed during the filming due to a dancer not looking their best, we got one, which did not always make the clock-watching producers happy. I learned what really works well on camera for dance. What Wayne did with *Dash*, as well as *Song & Dance* and *The Hot Shoe Show* in the 1980s, was way before its time when you look at the sensational dance shows of today.

During this furlough, I watched for any news of the Princess, whether it be newspaper articles or television coverage, to see how she looked. From what I could tell, she seemed to be thriving and it seemed her schedule was kept to mostly events in the U.K., including a visit to Glasgow, which I watched avidly. Wherever she went, the people lined the streets to catch a glimpse of this special lady.

I was excited to receive an official invitation from the Lord Chamberlain to a garden party at Buckingham Palace from 4 to 6 p.m. on Tuesday, July 10, 1984. This was what "coming to tea" meant. I laughed to myself at my ignorance, but it did feel special to be invited with my husband. I was quite sure invitees did not say they were unavailable to attend.

Of course, the biggest decision was what to wear, which was probably what all the other thousands of invited ladies were thinking. For men, it appeared to be much easier, choosing between morning dress, uniform, or lounge suit. Also attached to the invitation were the instructions on what to do upon arrival.

We got dressed and my daughter asked where we were going. I had the fun of telling her, "We are going to Buckingham Palace for tea with the Queen!" She thought that was funny.

As we arrived at the palace, we carefully followed the specific instructions, terrified that we might make a mistake. We parked our little car in the designated area and walked down the Mall to the gates of Buckingham Palace. There were people on either side of the street as we walked down its centre. It gave me just a tiny taste of what the Princess must experience on every one of her outings. The mood was joyous. We entered the famous palace gates and were directed up towards the magnificent building. The grandeur of the history swept over us, and the honour of the event filled us with pride as we passed through the interior of the palace and were directed outside to the royal gardens.

The first thing I noticed were the most stunningly beautiful flamingos prancing around; their vivid pink colour and their long necks were majestic. I felt wonderful in my pale peach silk dress and cream hat as we walked across the grass, which was a bit of a challenge in high heels. We approached the tents where tea was being served, the tables filled with elegant cucumber sandwiches, dainty cakes, strawberries, and sliced Victoria sponge cake on delicate plates with napkins. I was in my element. I love cake.

We walked around appreciating the gardens and admiring the hues and tones that the ladies wore and the variety of top hats and canes the gentlemen sported. The band played background music and then, when it played the national anthem, all fell silent as the Queen, the Princess, and several other members of the royal family made their way onto the lawn.

The entrance could not have been better choreographed. They separated individually down grass aisles warmly welcoming people. I was struck by their deep sense of duty. I'm not sure I would have liked three thousand people from all walks of life in my back garden, but they were nothing but gracious. The time seemed to go very quickly and the glorious afternoon left an indelible memory.

As September came round, something made me want to write a card to the Princess to let her know I was thinking of her. I knew the baby's birth must be close. I was not expecting a reply, but a letter arrived for me on September 15; it had been written the day before, which gave me a smile:

> *The last few weeks do tend to take forever and so when your message arrived it cheered me up no end!*
>
> *William has been saying for ages that the baby is cooked. I do tend to agree!*

The birth of Baby Wales Two was announced later that day. Henry Charles Albert David, affectionately to be known as "Harry," was born at 4:20 p.m. and weighed 6 lb. 14 oz. The very next day, a more confident Diana, now twenty-three, stepped out from the same hospital where William had been born, holding Harry in her arms, just as she had done with William, but this time looking a little more like an experienced mum.

CHAPTER EIGHT

Timing

I T WAS DECEMBER 1984 when I got the phone call from Anne-Beckwith Smith, followed by a letter laying out potential dates for dance classes. I had had major surgery that fall but knew I would be completely healed by the dates she suggested. There is nothing worse for a dancer than to stop moving and lie still, which was what the surgery had demanded. It certainly was an exercise in calming the mind. It was serendipity that my time in recovery coincided with the Princess's recovering from the birth of Harry.

At Christmas I received the royal Christmas card with the most beautiful family shot of the Prince and Princess with their two sons; it was signed by them both. I sat it proudly on the mantelpiece, along with the card from the previous year, which had been signed with much love from Diana.

A letter confirming the dates for the classes arrived and we were back in the studio at the end of January 1985. I couldn't wait to see Diana, and she threw her arms around me and embraced me warmly at our first class back. She looked to be in marvellous shape, although a little thinner, but that can be natural after giving birth, so I didn't think too much about it. You either fight to regain your shape or you are so busy that it drops off you on its own.

Diana swam regularly at the pool at Buckingham Palace. Although she admitted that she hated not being with the boys every minute possible, she thought it was a good way to get back in shape. She said William was wonderful with his little brother and she loved watching them together.

"Everyone seems very happy that we now have the heir and the spare! Harry's red hair was a lovely surprise as I know he's a Spencer as well as a Windsor," she said laughing. "My daddy is thrilled, but I'm not too sure what Charles thinks about that."

After asking me how I was and checking about my hospital stay, we went through our usual routine of warming up at the barre, followed by a few centring exercises for her stomach muscles. Stepping onto the main floor, we started with some simple side jazz chassés and back ball changes, then moving diagonally with free step ball changes, with arms swinging. I didn't want Diana to overdo it on the first class, but she was game, so we tackled some fan kicks into jazz pirouettes, which she enjoyed. "I feel wonderfully free and invigorated," she told me. "Thank you for always helping me, Anne. I feel I could tackle anything." It made me happy to know that dancing brought her this energy.

By late February 1985, I realized that I was pregnant and thought about what the best timing might be to tell Diana. Not that I had any intention of stopping classes, but I would probably start showing soon. With my first baby, I had continued performing up until the end of seven months and only stopped when I realized that getting up from a kneeling position on the floor, as I had to do as Mother to Clara in the first scene of *The Nutcracker*, was becoming extremely difficult. It neither looked nor felt elegant, and I knew then it was time to stop performances. Now, I was at the early stages of this pregnancy and stopping was still several months away. I was also going to Japan on the *Dash* tour with Wayne in March, followed by Europe, and I knew I would be showing by the time I got back.

I decided to tell Diana in late February, just before we were going to leave on tour. She received my news with warmth and, later that week, sent me a thoughtful letter, which read in part:

> *What wonderful news that baby Allan is on the way!*
>
> *I promise not to fuss but as a "mother of two" (!) I have every intention of keeping an eye on you during our lessons—so you have been warned. . .!*

It was uncanny that our timing so often worked out over the years. Recently, when I told someone I had danced with Diana, they asked the usual first question—"What was she like?"—and followed up with, "When did you teach her?" I smiled and said between 1981 and 1989, except when she was pregnant or I was pregnant, or she was on tour or I was on tour.

The Princess was scheduled to be on an official tour of Italy with her husband at the end of April. They would be visiting Florence, Milan, Venice, and Rome, which happened to coincide with me being in Rome with Wayne's show at approximately the same time. We had exchanged these details during our last class together in February. Diana joked as she said goodbye that day, saying, "See you in Rome!" It is those moments that I treasure most. No airs and graces, just a genuineness between us, as if we were good friends.

It was my first visit to Rome, and it was thrilling. Rehearsals took up a lot of the time, but when I did get out to sightsee, I was overwhelmed with the fact that I was standing amidst this land of ancient architecture, myth, and legend—and such great food! The streets were alive with families of all ages out together to enjoy their evening meals. The air was filled with delicious aromas, not to mention the sense of romance and love in such a beautiful setting. Perhaps the hormones of pregnancy had something to do with the allure, but I soaked it up.

Arriving at the theatre one evening, there was a telegram for me. Telegrams these days are unheard of. They were uncommon then, and this one was from the since-decommissioned Royal Yacht *Britannia*. I opened it and read.

Sad not to not have been able to see you in Rome, but wish you every possible success, with love, Diana.

Back on British soil at our next class in May, the Princess told me she had tried to change her schedule to come to see the performance in Rome, but it was too difficult as things were set and there was little free time. She looked quite tanned, although this was hard to gauge; she had told me her secret of using tanning oil on her legs to avoid wearing tights whenever possible. I did feel that Diana had lost weight and looked tired. I tried to gently address it, but she just said things had been extremely busy. I did not like to pry, but was concerned.

Diana and I danced every week through May and June and then the Season, as the British social calendar is known, was upon the Princess. The Season was originally designed for the presentation of debutantes at the royal court, until Queen Elizabeth II abolished that practice in 1958. By the 1980s, it was more inclusive of all members of society.

The highlights include the Chelsea Flower Show, a five-day event in May, held on the grounds of the Royal Hospital Chelsea. The Queen, who is patron of the Royal Horticultural Society, attends on the Monday before it opens to see the exquisite gardens. (These days, it is a favourite of King Charles III and Queen Camilla.) Royal Ascot follows in June, with each day of racing starting with members of the royal family arriving at the racetrack in a carriage procession. Everyone is expected to dress for the occasion. Ladies make statements in stunning hats. The men wear morning coats, full-length trousers, and immaculate shirts, usually adorned with the famous cravat known as the Ascot Tie. Wimbledon follows. It's the oldest tennis tournament in the world, dating back to 1877. It is a unique championship where the top international tennis players wear all-white outfits as they compete on grass courts. Diana loved this event.

Buckingham Palace garden parties would be held during the good weather of the season.

My husband and I had our second invite to a garden party on the same day as the previous year, July 10. This time, I was honoured to learn I would be presented to the Queen. I could hardly contain myself, and immediately worried about what dress would work with my six-month bump. My darling daughter asked once more where I was going. I told her tea with the Queen, and she said, "Again?!"

Knowing a little more of what to expect this time allowed me to enjoy the occasion more than the previous year. We were ushered into place at the front of a receiving line, with a select number of people, and were instructed to please stand there and wait for Her Majesty the Queen. When the Queen arrived, she made her way down the line, stopping to speak to each person. Her diminutive figure exuded presence and humbled me as she took my hand in her white-gloved hand in greeting, looking me directly in the eye. Her eyes were a charismatic blue and I remember marvelling at her porcelain skin: "How lovely to meet you, Anne." I curtsied and said the customary thank you, blown away that she knew my name. After a few words she moved on, and I watched as she took the time with each person to make them feel worthy. To do this on official engagements every single day of her life was not only admirable, but a lesson in discipline and duty. I knew I had just met a most remarkable woman.

By August, after the end of the Season, the Princess was in Balmoral for the annual summer vacation, and I was weeks away from giving birth. Diana had made me promise to let her know the minute the baby was born. My second beautiful daughter, Victoria, was born on September 2, 1985. On the next day, I received a letter from Diana with her congratulatory wishes:

> *One very wet and dull day was made all the happier on hearing the wonderful news that your little daughter has arrived safely and that you are both well.*
>
> *I long to see you both of course will wait to hear from you when we will next meet.*
>
> *With lots of love from us all.*
>
> *Diana.*

Many years later, when Victoria gave birth to her little one, my beautiful granddaughter Siena Rose, on January 15, 2020, I gave her the Princess's letter, which I had. I also gave her the red polka-dot baby's hairbrush-and-comb set that had been a gift from the Princess in honour of Victoria's birth. Diana had brought it when we returned to our classes that October.

CHAPTER NINE

A Change in the Air

IN OCTOBER, WE returned to the studio. I immediately felt a slight shift in Diana's demeanour; she seemed a little stressed and unhappy. As we went through the class, her mood lifted and she relaxed. At the end of the class, she said, "I'm so sorry I wasn't quite myself today but feel better now." I assured her that dancers go through many days where things don't go as well as they want, and not to worry. She then expressed what was troubling her. The constant press coverage was very difficult to handle. "I feel sure they are all just waiting on me to make more mistakes."

The press indeed was relentless, snapping photographs everywhere she went. She could not understand their fascination and much preferred to be left alone.

How could this beautiful lady be so unsure of herself? I quietly thought. I knew she had no idea how charismatic she was. That was her charm.

Diana's fall schedule was already filling up. The second official tour to Australia would be followed by the couple's first official visit to America in November, but before they left for abroad, a television interview of Diana and Charles aired. The response to the show, which also featured the children, was electric. People loved seeing what appeared to be a family living an idyllic life and indeed, at that time, it seemed to be just that. Although Diana had expressed to me that there were some things that she preferred in the way of music and fun that Charles didn't, she was still giddily in love, and more than anything wanted to please him and make him proud. The interview reaction did much to regain her confidence as she set out on the Australian tour.

When I got her postcard in the mail, I thought she sounded happy:

Our jet lag is quite awful and still after week we are walking around in a haze! I miss my dancing a lot and my boys.

From Australia, the couple flew to Washington, D.C., to start their American tour. It was a huge success. Americans fell in love with Diana and the now-iconic images of her and John Travolta dancing at the White House will never be forgotten. I was delighted to see that she had stretched her arms beautifully and lifted her head as she moved. I recognized the beginning of a new woman as she confidently danced with him. John knew how to partner and elegantly present his lady, which would have made it a lot easier for her to follow his moves. I'd seen her dance with Charles in Australia when she wore the stunning turquoise outfit with an emerald choker worn as a bandeau on her forehead. It was not as elegant. I had wished that they could have had a lesson together before that trip as Charles kept spinning her round, but she'd handled it remarkably well.

On her return to London, the Princess came bounding into the studio, to immediately tell me, "*I danced with John Travolta,*" and that it was the highlight of the whole tour. She absolutely loved it. That and sitting next to Mikhail Baryshnikov, but she was so in awe, she hardly spoke to him. "Everyone was so very kind to me and there were so many people everywhere, I really enjoyed the energy." We had a fun class that day trying out some disco moves with the hit tune "Stayin' Alive" from *Saturday Night Fever*.

Our conversation had taken us past our usual stop time. She spontaneously asked me where I was going after class. I told her to the subway at Hammersmith. "Why don't I drop you?" she said. I was startled. She then opened the studio door and told the detectives she was giving me a lift to the subway. I could tell they were not amused, and then she added that she was driving!

After we changed, we went to the car. I was put in the back seat and the Princess, laughing, took the wheel. The two detectives were still trying to change Diana's mind, but she had decided. It must have been a panic for the detectives on a security level.

The three detectives I knew best were Chief Inspector Graham Smith, Sergeant Allan Peters, and later the jovial Inspector Ken Wharfe. They were wonderful to me and always created a lighthearted atmosphere while fiercely protecting the Princess. They literally spent hours with Diana and were keenly alert. I knew they were not comfortable either with her driving or having me as her passenger. Diana was in her element, laughing, joking, knowing she was being naughty.

It was a few weeks after this that there was a much more serious incident that stopped any further car pranks. We had just started the class when one of the detectives came in to say that there was a car outside that they believed had followed them from Kensington Palace. They presumed it was press and they needed the Princess to get ready to leave quickly. The detective remained in the studio on a walkie-talkie to the other detective who was outside. I was told that I had to remain inside and wait there for some time after the Princess left. Diana dressed quickly and was rushed away within minutes.

I was aghast. I sat on the studio floor, unsure what to do. How long was "some time"? Would there be someone outside if I exited? My heart was racing. In the four years to date, we had never had a problem and were both rather proud of the fact that no one, except a few select people, knew the classes were taking place. It was not something I discussed. Yes, there were times that it would have been fun to share, but I never did.

I got dressed and decided to wait half an hour.

If this had happened today, I'm sure someone would have sent me a text to tell me when the coast was clear. But this was 1985. In many ways, I'm glad that iPhones and social media did not exist. Any photo of the Princess at that time was golden for the press, but for her, one of her in leotard and tights would have been detrimental.

It was the longest half hour I'd ever had to wait. I finally stepped tentatively outside. As I walked, I looked at every car, parked and moving, checking over hedges to see if anyone was following me. I decided to find the nearest café and sit and have a coffee, just to be sure I was not being followed. I had also had a shock. As I sat sipping a cappuccino, I hoped everything had gone smoothly for Diana.

About thirty minutes later I made my way to the subway and arrived home safely without incident, and hugged my daughters as soon I got in the door. It was probably just press looking for another exclusive, but for the detectives there must always have been the worry of a potential threat and danger to her. By the New Year, we had moved studios. Before that, though, there was the highlight of Christmas, 1985.

CHAPTER TEN

Uptown Girl

I
T WAS A few weeks before Christmas when Diana mentioned how lovely it would be to feel what it was like to do a performance.

In our dance classes, we had been building stamina by creating slightly longer and more difficult dance combinations, and now she had given herself permission to explore movement and not worry if it didn't quite work the first time. It was important to me that there were challenges, as well as fun.

Diana was much more comfortable with me watching her compared to the earlier classes in 1981, when she preferred that I danced beside her as a way of reminding her what the combo was, and because her shyness made it difficult for her to perform alone. She also found it hard to see herself in the mirror, which, as any dancer knows, is a good tool for learning. I would often reverse the position, so that she was facing away from the mirrors. It helped her to feel the dance from within. As we did this, her face would be aglow with emotion as she communicated without words the essence of her feeling.

When she mentioned the performance, I thought how important it was for dancers to have a goal, something specific to work on. At that moment, I had no idea that the performance she had in mind was on stage at Covent Garden, home of the Royal Ballet and the Royal Opera. As we talked a bit more about it, she said she thought it would be fun to perform at the Annual Friends Gala that took place every year around Christmas and was usually attended by royalty.

I gulped! That was a whole other world. I didn't know how to react.

I wasn't at all sure that it was a good idea, but as Diana talked on, I realized she had thought this all through down to choosing the music ("Uptown Girl" by Billy Joel) and who she wanted to dance with—Wayne Sleep. I could see the potential in the idea, knowing Wayne would be completely up for it and would create a memorable number. However, it would expose Diana in a very different light, performing in public. There already had been rumblings in the press that the many differences as to what Charles and Diana preferred in their lives were causing problems in their marriage—not that I paid a lot of attention to the press—but Diana herself had told me that Charles much preferred opera to dance, and that he didn't like her music. "Sometimes I find his friends all a bit stuffy," was how she put it, but she also made clear that he took his role of Prince of Wales very seriously. There were many issues that he had to deal with, she would say, while emphasizing how much she wanted to support him.

I decided to see if I could make this dream of hers happen. I invited Wayne to attend our next class at the studio. He was delighted to meet the Princess once again and to talk over her idea. I had given him an indication of what she was thinking, but let her tell him about her idea in her own way. Wayne thought the choice of song was brilliant, and I think he was somewhat relieved to discover this was to be more of a tongue-in-cheek number that would encourage the audience to have some fun.

Wayne had never seen Diana dance, so he was not sure of her capabilities. I knew this was the main concern for Wayne, and I was to make sure that Diana looked good and to choose steps that best showed her aptitude. Wayne spontaneously said, "Well, let's see what you can do!" Diana laughed at his boldness, but loved being treated as a dancer who was working with a choreographer. They had a wonderful rapport and a natural ease when dancing together.

For all of Wayne's lightheartedness, he was serious when it came to standards in dance. He felt he could make the number work by using the differences in their height to their advantage in a humorous way that would also fit with the lyrics to the song. Wayne was five foot two, and Diana was five foot ten.

The concept of the number was that they would play out the two characters in the story of the lyrics of the song. The Uptown Girl, Diana, was living in her upper-class world and the Downtown Boy, Wayne, was from a working-class family. She was tall, elegant, and very beautiful, and he was short, awkward, and did not think he was good-looking. Would the girl be interested in a boy like him? He had nothing but love to offer. He would bravely make a play and see.

We were now in November and the performance, which had already been scheduled for December 22, was a few weeks away. Wayne came to our next class to set the number, which was in a jazz style. It would start with him in virtuosic style so the audience would think it was going to be a special solo performance. He was much loved by the Royal Ballet audiences, and since he hadn't danced there for a while, this would set the mood. He would then present his partner and bring her onto the stage. Once the Uptown Girl made her entrance, they would start dancing together. There was a lot of humour in the number. It was also going to be demanding on a technical level with many high kicks and turns. These would have to be perfected. Wayne gave me permission to slightly adjust his choreography should there be anything that looked too cumbersome or awkward.

Given that it was the Christmas season, Wayne was scheduled to rehearse and perform in a pantomime. This meant we could only fit in one more rehearsal with him before the actual day of the event.

Pantomime has a huge history in Britain. Shows are performed at the Christmas season for a few weeks only, usually based on a fairy tale, and include lots of songs, jokes, and slapstick comedy. They are designed to make children laugh. Very often the audience is asked to participate by shouting out if the villain appears. Wayne loved the happy atmosphere and the larger-than-life costumes, usually playing the role of the Dame. He was always a huge hit with the audience.

I want to point out that the rehearsals we had did not take place at Kensington Palace, as indicated on Netflix's *The Crown*, but in the dance studio where we had been working out since 1981. But I did know that Diana loved dancing down the hallways of her Kensington Palace home, as she had mentioned this to me. And like our classes, the most important thing was that no one should know that the live performance was being planned. It needed to be a complete surprise for the audience and Charles, who would be sitting in the royal box. How then were we going to rehearse on the Covent Garden stage, a very different ambiance from a studio, and keep this a secret? It was decided we would have to tell a few key people.

A couple of days before the performance, we told Leslie Edwards, who was supervising the event. Leslie was now the esteemed ballet master for the Royal Ballet, after a distinguished career as a dancer. He was elated. "How marvellous," he said. "What can I do to help?" He was such a gentleman and discreet in how he organized our rehearsal, first in the dance studio of the Royal Opera House and then a short rehearsal on stage on the day of the show. For the latter, he cleared everyone in the house to ensure our privacy. He knew how important it was for the performers to feel comfortable on this historic stage, nearly 2,500 square feet in size and looking out on a 2,500-seat auditorium. It was going to be daunting. The dancing duo also needed to have a chance to practice with the lighting cues, which could be blinding. There was a series of turns at the end of the number that required great focus from both dancers, and they would have to adjust their eyes to the lighting.

The inclusion of their dance number in the program was referred to as the "Special Item." No names were mentioned. When asked about it, Leslie would say, "Oh, Sleep's doing something." The dance was positioned as the penultimate number, which meant the Princess had to sit through most of the performance. This concerned me, as she would need time to warm up and, if she had to wait that long, chances were good that her nerves would get the better of her.

We also told Ken Davidson, who was a high-up administrator for the company, about her appearance so that he could ensure the proper security was in place. This was made a little easier by the fact that royalty was expected that evening, but he would have to ensure that additional detectives were placed backstage as well.

I'd suggested that Diana wear her performance dress for the rehearsal. She had chosen the dress herself and I hadn't yet seen it, but we needed to check it to be sure there weren't any potential wardrobe malfunctions. We certainly didn't want any embarrassing mishaps. It was also important that Wayne know the feel of the material and the length of her dress in preparing for doing the lifts. The dress was rather low cut with thin straps, which meant she would not be wearing a bra, and that was a concern. There was no time to fit her with "cookies," as they are endearingly called in the dance world, which are strapless covers for the breasts, a technique that most dancers use for safety.

I was also worried about her shoes, which were low heeled and slip-ons. What if they were to fall off her feet mid-lift? So, when I went home to change after the rehearsal, I quickly mustered up two wide elastic bands that could be worn around her shoes to ensure there was no danger of that happening. I applied pancake make-up onto the elastics so that they matched her tights. The elastics were not very elegant, but the worry over safety far outweighed how they looked, and since they were on stage, nobody would really be looking too closely, or so I thought.

The studio rehearsal saw two giggling performers trying to go through their number. In true Wayne fashion, he had forgotten half the steps he had set a few weeks before, but then quickly pulled things together. I stood back, shaking my head, wondering what was going to happen during the show. But they were having the best time. Things went better during the stage rehearsal, during which Leslie Edwards turned to me and said, "She's rather good," which was a relief to hear. They were prepared as much as they could be, and I had to trust that it would go well.

That evening, I arrived backstage at the theatre and was greeted by Keith, the stage manager, who had to be in the loop of people knowing so that he could run his stage efficiently. Keith and I had worked together before, so I was relieved and knew we were in good hands. I had been backstage for performances when I was a student and knew the area well. He invited me to stand in the downstage corner of the wings until I was needed.

The plan was that the Princess would slip out of the royal box and I would meet her in the King's Smoking Room, where we would get her changed on time to connect with Wayne and head to the stage at the last moment. She could not be away too long from the royal box—that would be suspicious. As things got started, I tried to enjoy watching the performances from the wings, but it seemed like an eternity until the scheduled moment.

Finally, when I went to get her, Diana was already in the King's Smoking Room. She told me she couldn't sit in the box a minute longer.

She was pacing and eating at a voracious rate from the table, which was covered in goodies. She was very hyper. I took her to change and was glad that Wayne was there when we got back so we could both calm her a little. Adrenaline is good for performance, but not quite that much!

She couldn't relax, so Wayne and I decided that we should take her to the stage area, even though it was rather early. She would then have a feel for the performance energy. Artists backstage greeted her with surprised smiles. She began to enjoy the electric atmosphere of the gala. I took her hand and smiled at her in a way to say that we both knew she was about to fulfill a childhood dream of dancing at Covent Garden.

When the music started and Wayne entered the stage, the audience went wild with approval. He performed in his singular style starting with a series of coupé jeté en manège, as he travelled around the stage with great virtuosity, then came to the centre for a series of fast à la seconde turns. The audience offered enthusiastic support. He then travelled to the wing and gestured that he was presenting someone. As instructed, Diana waited a moment before entering to build the excitement.

When she entered, there was an audible intake of breath from the audience. Diana quickly and confidently completed her first steps of a jazz strut across the stage, and a thunderous applause erupted. The audience could not believe what they were seeing. She had been choreographed to stop for two bars of music, look at the audience, give a couple of jazz shoulder rolls when she saw the Downtown Boy, then continue with some jazz slides to see if he was following. The Downtown Boy, catching up with her, took her hand, then twirled her round; she reciprocated, twirling him, then showing she could do more turns, doubled the turning. Next was her favourite moment, placing her hands on Wayne's head and pushing him down into a kneeling position, then kicking one of her legs high over his head. The audience loved the storytelling of the move. He then rose and followed her around the stage, finally sweeping her up in a lift in his arms and carrying her diagonally across the stage. When Wayne put Diana down from the lift, it was time for the big finish.

The two dancers made their way around both sides of the stage to meet upstage center and join hands stretched out to the side in a series of high kicks coming straight down centre stage towards the audience, in true Broadway style. Finally, Diana ran to the left corner downstage, near the exit, as if she was about to leave Wayne behind with the decision of whether to follow her. The Downtown Boy asked the audience with a wink: Should he go after her? With much laughter from the audience, he joined her, and they both ran off stage, joyous and breathless. Diana went through the routine flawlessly, and with true performance spirit. It was a performance of a lifetime for both.

The audience loved every second of it, calling for more and breaking into whistles, cheers, and applause. Everyone who had been watching backstage joined the clapping spontaneously.

The dancing couple went back out for their curtain calls and had to take several, till Wayne decided that was enough. "Let's leave them wanting more," he said. As she came off from the final bow, Diana said to both of us, "Beats the wedding!"

Wayne and I were astounded.

Diana was on a high when she came off stage. She was thrilled with the reaction from the audience and that she had danced so well. She grabbed my hand and pulled me along as we made our way back to the private room to change for the reception. She literally dropped her costume to the floor in front of me and, without batting an eye, did a quick underarm clean-up and donned her beautiful red velvet dress with a change of shoes. As I was zipping her up, she applied a touch of compact powder to her face and was ready to step out to meet people.

As we were led to the reception area where Charles would be, we passed many members of the audience who congratulated her, which she truly loved. She smiled back at every one, her cheek still a little flushed from dancing, but glowing with the knowledge that her performance had been a success. She made her way to Charles, and as she stood before him, I could sense she desperately wanted his approval. He said, "Well done, darling," and turned to talk with someone else. I sensed disapproval from him and my heart took a thud. Some other guests did tell her what a surprise it had been and how much they loved the performance, but I was acutely conscious of those from the royal circle who did not say anything to her and looked down their nose at me, their disapproval evident.

As they left, the Princess hugged me and said she would never forget this evening. I was very happy for her and knew she had experienced something unique. Something truly hers. I hoped there would not be any unwanted attention about the performance, but, of course. it hit the papers the next day. The press had arrived at the theatre just as the final curtain was coming down and unbeknownst to Wayne and me, there had been a photographer shooting throughout the number. Those were the images that made headlines.

I never did discover how the photographer learned of the performance. Luckily, I was given the photographs by George Lawson, Wayne's manager, who managed to procure copies for me. A stamp on the back of each read "copyright by Reg Wilson," a photographer known for shooting theatrical moments and capturing the motion of dance. Of course, when I looked at the photographs, all I could see were the bloody shoe elastics, which were never supposed to be noticed.

CHAPTER ELEVEN

New Studios and Growing Pressures

SINCE CHRISTMAS WAS just a few days after the premiere performance of *Diana and Wayne*, we agreed we would meet again after the holidays, which Diana would be spending at Windsor Castle. Not her favourite place in the world, she told me, as she was always cold, although not quite as cold as she was at Balmoral—"It really doesn't stop raining in Scotland, does it, Anne?" she asked. I had to agree.

In January 1986, we were scheduled to meet to resume classes. There had been a lot of press after the Covent Garden night, which provoked questions about Diana and her dancing. This event, coupled with the incident when Diana's car was followed to Merle Park's studio, prompted the Palace to change our dance class venue.

The location was tremendously helpful for both of us as the new studios were at the rehearsal rooms of the London Festival Ballet, located next door to the Royal Albert Hall. This meant the Princess was very near to her home at Kensington Palace and could be there and back in a very short time. It made my travel a lot easier, too. I loved getting out at the Piccadilly stop, reminding myself of that first meeting with Anne Beckwith-Smith at The Ritz as I went by, followed by a short bus ride down the road that passed Kensington Gardens on the right and the Royal Albert Hall, home to the BBC's Proms concerts, on the left. The Albert Memorial monument, which commemorates Queen Victoria's husband, stands opposite the Royal Albert Hall. The ornate statue of Albert shows him holding the catalogue of the 1851 Great Exhibition in his hands; at his feet are carved figures depicting painters, sculptors, architects, and musicians. An inspiration to anyone.

The entrance to the studios of the London Festival Ballet, which came to be known as the English National Ballet under the artistic direction of Peter Schaufuss, was down a quiet lane at the back of the building. Perfect for the royal car to arrive privately, allowing the detectives to view anyone coming and going as they pulled up to the back doors. There were two studios that we used at different times. The upstairs one was very large with a feeling of grandeur, and the downstairs one was smaller and more intimate, which we grew to love. Diana could step straight out from the parked car at the back doors of the studio, letting the doors fly open with panache, opening her coat to reveal herself already dressed in dance gear. She would announce herself with a drum roll flair, laughing profusely. If anyone had seen her, it would have made a fabulous news clip; fortunately, no one did.

During our first class in the new location, Diana reiterated how much she had loved the feeling of performance and that her debut at Covent Garden had kept her smiling all through Christmas. She admitted that she didn't think Charles thought it appropriate, with a bit of a naughty grin on her face. He had not liked her showing herself in that way.

As we continued our classes over the next few months, enjoying our new studios and lessons together, Diana began to express to me her frustration with the press. She found the constant coverage difficult to manage, especially since the press took photos at every inconceivable moment. "The reporters keep calling my name until I turn to look, when I am trying to focus on what I am supposed to be doing at that moment, then all I see is flashing cameras. It's like I'm under a microscope being examined, it makes me feel so uncomfortable. They are all just waiting for me to make a terrible blunder." I sympathized with her and reassured her she was doing an amazing job.

It was in March when, to my horror, for the first time, I was late for the class, although I didn't know it until I arrived. Having always been in the studio at least twenty minutes before the scheduled time, on this day I arrived to find the Princess sitting on the barre, her back against the mirror, legs crossed and swinging to and fro. Her detective was with her. She laughed when I came in—my face must have been a picture. "You thought it was 9:30 today," she said. I had indeed, but she had 9 a.m. in her calendar. It was about ten minutes after nine. Seeing my huge embarrassment, Diana slipped off the barre and said, "Come on, I'm taking you back to mine for tea. They are going to announce Fergie's engagement and I want to see it." Adding, "It will be such a relief to have the attention on Fergie rather than me."

The detectives must have been warned of her plan because they smiled and opened the backseat door of the car for me so I could sit next to the Princess. We entered through the famous gates at Kensington Palace, my mind in a whirl. Arriving at the back entrance of her home at the palace, Diana bolted up the stairs, taking me with her. Her butler warmly welcomed us when we got to the apartment, and I found myself standing in a very cozy sitting room with beautiful dusty-pink couches. Diana rushed to put the television on, asking for some tea at the same time. The butler was very relaxed, and the Princess had a lovely interaction with him as she introduced me. (I don't remember it being Paul Burrell; I believe he became her butler a year later, in 1987.)

Diana invited me to sit down beside her on the pink couch. She kicked off her shoes, sank into the comfy cushions, and watched the announcement with contagious excitement. She was thrilled with the coverage and happy to have a friend in the royal circle. Sarah Ferguson's bubbly personality and less formal approach was appealing to Diana. The butler brought the tea and Diana thanked him and then did the pouring. We sipped it while enjoying the coverage, Diana continuing to speak of what a relief it was to have someone with whom she could connect and how she looked forward to the wedding and having the attention on Andrew and Fergie. We checked different channels, taking it all in. The engaged couple looked extremely relaxed and happy. Fergie's red ruby ring, surrounded by ten diamonds, dazzled. It suited her outgoing personality.

I was unsure how long to stay, but there came a lull in the conversation after about fifty minutes. I took that as my cue, as it would be around the time our class would have finished. Diana and I said goodbye, and I thanked her for this special time. I was then escorted to the entrance of the house to take my leave. I was on a high as I walked out to the palace gates and through the park.

I had tried to take as much of it in as I could while I was there, but it was a bit mind-blowing, even though I had been made to feel quite welcome. I confess that I rushed home and called my mother to tell her I had tea with Diana at Kensington Palace. She said, "Lovely, dear, was the tea hot?" My mother hated a cup of tea that was not.

The friendship with Fergie often got Diana into trouble. She told me about their adventure when they dressed up as police, and I could see how much fun it had been for her. It must have been a great relief for her to have someone her own age and newly married to chat with. When their pranks went a bit far, she was reminded by the Palace that she was the future queen and should behave accordingly. She said it was like being told off by the headmistress. She dutifully listened and promised to be better behaved.

Diana was beginning a gruelling schedule, with many engagements that would be followed by tours to Canada and Japan. Our dance classes would take a small hiatus if she was out of the country. She was not looking forward to being away from her sons again. It was becoming increasingly more difficult to have quality time with them, she told me. They were still just four and not quite two and she felt they needed their mum: "Being with my boys is so important to me." I totally understood as I felt the same about my daughters. I could tell that the endless commitments were wearing on Diana, but she never cancelled a scheduled visit; she did not want to disappoint people. "I must always give my very best," she said.

Diana fainted while visiting Expo 86 in Vancouver with Charles. That concerned me. She had looked quite thin before leaving Britain, and it raised my suspicions that she might have an eating disorder. Prior to going, Diana had expressed how difficult she found eating at receptions, as there was so much chatting coupled with intense scrutiny and pressure to live up to what people expected of her. I gently approached the subject of her well-being, and she assured me she was fine, just a bit overwhelmed, and thanked me for being concerned.

The Japanese portion of the visit further showed the immense popularity of the couple, with the focus more on Diana. She still found time amidst the hectic schedule to send me a postcard:

> It's a wonderful country and people have been so kind.
> The time change has left us in a complete daze! Chopsticks have been a disaster and how I long for a bowl of Shreddies!!

All these years later, we have become aware of all the wonderful hand-written letters and postcards Diana sent to so many people. She had her own humorous style and often added an emoji before they were popular, which was sure to make the receiver smile. I thought about how much time this correspondence would take out of her day, and the discipline required to do it; she would never go to bed if she had not completed her thank-you notes. Diana was thoughtful and caring. She wanted very much to ensure her appreciation was felt.

CHAPTER TWELVE

Come See the Cabaret!

S ARAH FERGUSON AND Prince Andrew's wedding took place on July 23, 1986. A week or so later, Diana asked me about Wayne's new role in the musical *Cabaret*, which recently opened at the Strand Theatre in London's West End.

Wayne was playing the legendary role of the MC, Master of Ceremonies, originally played by Joel Grey both on stage and in the acclaimed movie. This new production was directed and choreographed by Gillian Lynne, whose choreography of the hit musical *Cats* had been integral to the success of that show. I admired Gillian greatly and had the pleasure of meeting her earlier in the year. She was looking for a classically trained dancer who could help with the research of dancers at the Paris Opera for the upcoming production of *The Phantom of the Opera*. Wayne had kindly suggested me, and we had an instant rapport. Diana said that she would love to see Wayne in performance. I told her that, although the title indicated a highly entertaining, fun evening, *Cabaret* was in fact a dark musical with a disturbing storyline as cabaret was a metaphor for the political scene in 1931 Berlin and the increasing popularity of the Nazi Party.

I knew from Wayne that Gillian's vision for the production was in a Brechtian style. She wanted a more authentic reality, with a seedy nightclub, as depicted in Christopher Isherwood's semi-autobiographical novel upon which the musical was based. The dancing style was extremely suggestive and decadent. I knew Gillian would have no fear of showing that in her choreography. Anyone who has worked with this incredible lady will have heard her shout out in rehearsal, "Nipples up, everyone!!" The sometimes acutely embarrassed cast would nonetheless dutifully comply.

For Wayne, the role of MC was more acting and singing than dance, which was usually what people loved about him and came to the theatre to see. Gillian added as much dance as she could without interfering with the truth of the character. Wayne played the role with a lovable flamboyance, but a sinister presence. "I'm not sure that Wayne will be recognizable to you!" I told Diana. "I would still love to go and maybe we could have dinner afterwards," she said. Asking her what she might like to eat, she told me, "Oh, just pizza. I love pizza." Then she added, "Bring your husband. I'd love to meet him."

And so it happened.

It was more of a fun evening out than an official engagement. That sounds simple enough, but there was a great deal that went into a night out for the Princess of Wales. At the outset, we had to reserve tickets for the show. The tickets were allocated for specific seats, which meant the box office knew who was coming—there had to be enough seats for the entourage that would come with the Princess. The detectives did a sweep of the theatre prior to the show, both backstage and in the front of house, which threatened to disrupt our schedules. Everything needs to be in place for a performance before what's known as *the half,* a sacrosanct thirty-minute stretch before the curtain goes up. The actors use the half to quietly prepare; the front-of-house staff meanwhile open the doors, allowing the audience time to be comfortably seated. The detectives insisted on doing the sweep right before the half, when everyone backstage was rushing to get things done. The tech guys, in particular, were irritated, but they softened later when they learned why.

As had been arranged, my husband was already seated right behind where the Princess would sit. I would join him once the Princess was seated and we would be flanked by two security officers, giving the protection team easy access to her if needed. Diana and I arrived at the last minute, having travelled in the car together, and slipped into the assigned seats as the lights were going down. At the intermission, she was quickly escorted out to a private room for refreshments, then brought back as the entr'acte was playing.

I'm not sure how many people around us saw the performance that night. Of course, they recognized Diana and watched her more than the stage.

When the performance was over, the Princess was taken backstage, which she always loved to do. Behind the curtain, she met the cast, who were still in their sexy costumes and haunting make-up. They were thrilled to meet her, and she chatted away, enjoying every minute of it. Finally, we left by the stage door and encountered the usual frenzy. Audience members had gathered at the door and vied for her attention. She took the time to good-naturedly tell everyone how much she enjoyed the show. Press photographers got some shots, too.

Afterward, we went to an Italian restaurant where George and Wayne had organized a private room for dinner. My husband and I travelled in a car that followed the Princess's car to the restaurant. Wayne came later, after he had changed, as did Gillian and her husband, Peter Land, who had played Chris in the production. I was happy to have the chance to have dinner with Gillian and to get to know her better, as we had agreed that I would be working with her when we were in rehearsals for *Phantom* in September. I hoped she would understand when I told her that I may have to miss a couple of hours out of the morning rehearsal each week, but I wasn't going to mention that just yet.

Once we were all seated around a large table, with the Princess taking her seat first at the head of the table, drinks were offered and polite chatter ensued. Then several waiters entered with lidded silver serving platters. In perfect precision, ten pizzas were revealed. I had told George and Wayne what Diana had suggested we eat and they had ordered ahead. The Princess laughed at the presentation. Everyone laughed. Apparently, I was the only one who had taken "just pizza" seriously. The joke was on me. The pizzas were whisked away (Diana later insisted on paying for them), and everyone ordered off the menu. Nevertheless, the pizzas broke the ice for a fun evening.

I received a letter thanking me for organizing her night on the town. I loved her honest comment that the show was "interesting," which confirmed what I already knew—*Cabaret* was not her cup of tea:

> *I had the most wonderful evening with lots of laughter . . .*
>   *I thought the actual show was very "interesting" but still feel that Wayne may need more of a challenge, who am I to know though?!*

CHAPTER THIRTEEN

The Essence of Dance

W HEN YOU DANCE, the way you feel very often affects the way you hold your body. Before our night out to see *Cabaret,* there was a day when the Princess arrived at the studio, and I instantly knew something was wrong. She was gracious about trying to throw it off, and we started gently into our routine.

Often dance can do much to shift your frame of mind, and in my acute awareness of Diana's sad energy, I wanted to lift her out of herself and make her feel better. The concentration that is required to focus on movement can help the brain switch to thinking only of the physical task. We started an adagio and began to stretch our bodies slowly, letting the blood flow more easily. When we do this in dance, a warmth starts from within. As we practised the lyrical combination of steps, she started to relax through the language of movement. We repeated the adagio a few more times, and I watched, without being intrusive.

The freedom of movement in dance allows an expression of true feeling, which is separate from the technique of dance. One transcends technique and joins in the emotion of the movement. This separate expression is what truly makes the dancer. Have you ever seen a performance and found it deeply moving? That is because you are experiencing the *emotion in motion,* the essence of dance. It lives deep in the dancer's soul and, when it is expressed, the audience can feel it. As I was the audience member that day, I was moved.

At the end of the dance moment, Diana sat on the floor with tears in her eyes, and an outpouring of emotion followed. There had been times during our class over the years, and as early as 1982, where Diana had shared some of the difficulties that she was going through. This time it was different. I could feel the hurt, a helplessness within her. She was very accepting of my comfort, in between saying, "You must think me awful." I didn't.

I asked if she wanted to share what was making her feel so sad, but also told her if she just needed to cry and sit for a while that was perfectly fine. I had never seen Diana like this before, although I had seen her upset.

One of the early conversations we had had was that she desperately wanted her children to experience everyday life and have a broader outlook on the world. She shared with me the disagreements that it caused with her husband as William's schooling was being decided. Charles's experience at school had been very difficult. At thirteen he had been sent to the remote boarding school of Gordonstoun, which then had an austere and strict atmosphere designed to toughen up young men for adulthood. Although it was still some years away, she wanted to carve out a different experience for her children, and preferably schools somewhere close to her until William was ready to leave the nest.

Diana's choice of Wetherby School in London's Notting Hill as a pre-preparatory school offered a more forward-thinking, kind, caring, individual approach, which she felt would best suit William's temperament. She was relieved when she won what she felt was another battle, one that she wished she didn't have to fight. She worried that the "establishment" found her difficult.

Slowly, after a few more minutes of gentle sobbing, she said, "I just can't seem to do anything right when it comes to my husband. I do love him so much and want him to be proud of me, but I don't think he feels the same way." I just let her talk, not offering advice, but just listening. She continued, "I don't understand why I am not enough for him; I think he prefers an older woman."

There had been tongue-in-cheek comments previously about her thinking her husband was visiting another lady, as she put it, which was hard to hear. But those comments had appeared to be suspicions only, so I had reassured her and reminded her how beautiful she was. This time it was clearly out in the air and needed a response. I asked her why she felt that. What followed was very alarming to hear. "I know he is seeing Camilla again. Am I expected to accept that, like the other Princesses of Wales before, one just turns a blind eye to husbands having a mistress! Why does he not love me? I really don't understand. I have tried everything, tried to conform to his wishes even though I don't always agree. There's no affection between us, and I am always on my own. I just want to be loved. I can't keep going on like this. They are really expecting me to just say nothing and keep going. How do I do that?"

It was like a friend talking to me about a very difficult relationship they were in and looking for advice and, more importantly, looking for a better understanding of how they got to be where they found themselves. I must stress that the knowledge we now have of the relationship Charles had with Camilla Parker Bowles did not exist at that time. Today, the public believes it knows everything about the demise of their marriage—there has been so much said in newspaper articles, interviews, documentaries, and television series. Diana herself eventually told her personal story, but that was not until Andrew Morton's book of 1992, followed by the controversial Martin Bashir interview of 1995, on which she said, "There were three of us in this marriage, so it was a bit crowded." Both interviews came very many years after this moment in time. Diana would have to live through a great deal more before finally speaking out.

It is a very different thing when someone is going through the discoveries of deceit as they are happening: the hurt, pain, confusion, anger, and finally resolution, if possible. This was no ordinary situation, especially given Diana's job of always having to be on, and having her every move, her conduct and demeanor, scrutinized in the press. Comportment was an important part of being Her Royal Highness the Princess of Wales. There would be several other conversations in the future, but in this moment in 1986, I tried to help to heal a wound, to bandage it up so it could have time to heal. But it would leave a scar.

CHAPTER FOURTEEN

Grace and Gratitude

I WAS MOST ANXIOUS to see the Princess the following week and hoped that things were feeling better for her. It had been a hard week for me, as my mind kept returning to our conversation. The last thing I wanted was for Diana to feel any embarrassment being back in the studio, so I approached the week's class with a warm energy.

Diana came bouncing into the room and we got to work. I felt very pleased that she was comfortable. I thought it a huge compliment of trust that nothing was said about last week's conversation. I told the Princess I had a new song for her and played Lionel Richie's new single "Dancing on the Ceiling," which she loved. We laughed a lot and got a very good sweat going that day.

At the end of the class as she was leaving, she gave me a yellow envelope as she waved goodbye. Inside was a beautiful card. It had an image of a teddy bear. "People like me," it said on the front and, on the inside, "like people, like you V. much." Diana had written:

Words are inadequate to what I feel but you know how deeply I appreciate your advice.

CHAPTER FIFTEEN

New Beginnings

A NEW HAIRCUT CAN do a lot for a woman. And that's what happened with the Princess of Wales.

She was about to go on a nine-day tour to Oman, Qatar, Bahrain, and Saudi Arabia in November 1986, and the heat in the region would be intense. Shorter hair would be an advantage, but the real reason behind it was that Diana wanted a change. She had decided that she would take on a new look and, in so doing, assert herself as the new woman she was becoming.

"Shy Di" was the nickname the press had given her, and that part of her would always be there, but she was proving that when you can find courage despite the fear you feel, a new strength develops within you. This meant allowing herself to trust in the value and importance of the work she did, finding and acknowledging the causes that she cared deeply about, and that were shaping her more and more. The young Princess that I had first met now stood taller and set out boldly. She was going to make the role of Princess of Wales matter. She looked magnificent as she and Charles began their tour, her carefully chosen wardrobe showing British fashion of the highest standard. The trip was a huge success.

There had been a new beginning for me as well, as I had started rehearsals for *The Phantom of the Opera.* At the time, I had no idea of the new life it would bring me in the years ahead.

I would be working with the renowned musical score of the legendary composer Andrew Lloyd Webber and a creative team with exceptional standards, led by the genius of Hal Prince. From the first day, I was in awe. My role was to assist Gillian Lynne in all the choreography and staging of the production and, most importantly, to spend time with the singer, actress, and dancer Sarah Brightman to prepare her for the dance aspects in her role as Christine Daaé. This meant she had to play one of the ballet dancers of the Paris Opera Ballet chorus, which required her to dance en pointe. It was essential for the story line that these ballet scenes were believable.

I had enjoyed doing the research for the production, studying Edward Degas' drawings as he so identified with the subject of ballet and the human expression within the art. The difference in the technical style, where the body is pitched slightly forward and the arms and hands delicately held to frame the dancer's face and body, were to be incorporated into the choreography. Prior to rehearsals, I worked in a studio with Gillian as she brilliantly created the style, mood, and lives of the dancers, both on and off stage, and that of the austere ballet mistress Madame Giry, played by Mary Millar.

The second act was to open with a masked ball; the title of the first number was "Masquerade." This number was tremendously challenging as it was to include the whole company, who were placed on a magnificent, curving staircase, which took up most of the stage area. Everyone was to wear a mask, which had its own challenges for the performers, who had to descend the steps while singing but without looking down. In addition, life-sized dummies were placed on the stairs so the audience would think there were vast numbers of people at this ball. As the curtain went up on the spectacular frozen image of colourful characters, it was hard to know who was human and who was not. Gillian started the number with a sharp doll-like movement and the dummies moved slightly when touched.

The iconic mask that the designer Maria Björnson had magnificently conceived to cover half of the Phantom's disfigured face inspired Gillian to represent it in movement, as he was the central character and his existence was feared by all. I will never forget the day Gillian arrived in the studio and said, "I've got it!" She dove into showing me the movement that would accompany the first lyric of the famous "Masquerade" number: each person on stage would sharply raise their hand to cover half of their face to replicate the image of the mask, then slowly extend their hand straight up to reveal who they were. And so it was born, that first accent, with an indelible image, before the words sang out "Masquerade! Paper faces on parade."

Gillian also wanted to enhance the dance component of the show as much as she could. Having Sarah play Christine seemed to speak out for it. With that thought in mind, we were due to meet quietly with Andrew to discuss the possibility of including a section just for the ballet dancers that would give a solo dancing moment to Sarah. Composers are not always willing to change what they have already written, and they don't want to feel they are being coerced to do so. But Andrew was open to Gillian's suggestion and, after rehearsal one evening, we were to meet Andrew in what Gillian and I would term the inner sanctum! It was a small private room with a beautiful grand piano on which Andrew sometimes composed. When we entered, Andrew was sitting at the piano, gently playing. It was wonderful to see him in his own world, completely at one with the keys. We did not interrupt till he finished. He was then very welcoming.

Gillian's idea was to insert a musical bridge for the dancers in "Masquerade" that would allow Sarah to shine, as the Phantom watched her longingly from a hidden place. Gillian described her vision for the middle of the number: no singing, just music, and this would be the moment when Sarah would be highlighted. Gillian and Andrew were both inspiring to watch as they created the music together. We left feeling ecstatic at the achievement.

The next day, Gillian choreographed the new dance section for Sarah, having worked out the steps with me. Sarah was an extremely hard worker who took up the challenge with determination. She had been one of the members of Hot Gossip, the troupe of sexy jazz dancers that Arlene Phillips had created. Now she had to become a demure ballet girl and be convincing. Sarah had early ballet training, but she hadn't touched pointe work in years. We had been slowly building her technique in our private dance sessions and her pointe work was getting strong.

When we were ready, we brought Andrew in to see the completed new choreography. He loved this chance to see his new wife, Sarah, rehearse this addition to his work. Unfortunately, by the time we were ready to put it together with the cast, we were told that it was going to be cut. That is often the hardest and most ruthless part of doing a new musical. Sections are often cut to save time or to protect the flow of the story. But Gillian knew how to compromise. She fought to keep half the new choreography, and she won.

I now had to ask Gillian if I could have a few hours off each week. When I did, she looked at me in disbelief. Requesting time off during rehearsals is usually a strong no, and any professional knows you should never miss any rehearsal, especially when assisting the choreographer, for fear of missing the specific moment when something extraordinary is created.

Gillian was quite taken aback until I explained that the classes were for the Princess of Wales. She had no knowledge that I was teaching her until that moment. Wayne had always kept it confidential. I had to ask Gillian for the same confidentiality, which she agreed to, saying, "I suppose it's a royal command, so of course you must." She later told me that she was delighted for me, and that her country home in Gloucestershire was very close to the Princess's home. She loved having her as a neighbour.

Diana was enthralled hearing about the rehearsal process for *Phantom* and it was a joy to share as much as I could with her without giving too much away. Having asked me about Michael Crawford, who was playing the Phantom, I was able to tell her about the remarkable day when we were all invited to sit in on one of the Phantom's rehearsals, which had been strictly "closed doors" to that point, with only a few necessary people allowed in the room.

Michael was well known for his huge comedic skills, particularly in the hit TV show *Some Mothers Do 'Ave 'Em,* in which he played a haphazard man who caused disasters wherever he went, and in the West End show *Billy.* But he gained the biggest acclaim for his brilliant physical stunts in the musical *Barnum,* based on the life of Phineas Taylor Barnum, the founder of the Barnum & Bailey Circus. To perform them, he had trained at circus school.

The role as the Phantom was a complete contrast, as it was a dramatic role with an operatic score. There was much skepticism about whether Michael would be able to pull it off vocally. Gillian had told me he had been taking coaching from the renowned Ian Adam, who was also Sarah's voice teacher.

You could hear a pin drop as the scene in the Phantom's lair began. Those in attendance, the whole company and the creatives, were sitting tensely. Michael began to sing "Music of the Night," which the Phantom sings to lure Christine to his lair, his voice almost putting her in a trance. The performance was mesmerizing; the emotion he brought into the room was palpable. We knew that we were amidst something that was going to be extraordinary. There was complete silence when the scene was finished, followed by an explosion of sheer disbelief and admiration. Michael had not only sung it magnificently, but his acting had brought the room to tears.

Michael smiled and was humbled as he received the company's appreciation of his brilliance. He had set a standard of excellence for the whole company, inspiration for all of us. When I told the Princess, she was moved, immediately recognizing the pressure that he must have been under. Perhaps that was something that resonated with her.

When it came to the technical rehearsals on stage for *Phantom*, there were many challenges. It was a long process to get the show ready, given the number of performers, costuming, music, and staging.

I had been sitting in the dress circle with Gillian as we watched the technical rehearsal of the travellator (or moving walkway) that was to be timed to the music. The device was needed to move a mechanical horse that the Phantom and Christine would ride to reach the boat that would take them to the Phantom's secret lair. The horse was nicknamed Dobbin by the two of us in one of our giddier late-night dress rehearsals. Gillian and I both knew it was not going to work and frustration was building—so much time was being spent getting the device to function properly. Finally, after Dobbin had careered down the travellator for the umpteenth time, we were relieved to hear Hal shout at the top of his voice, "Cut the horse!"

In its place, the Phantom, holding a lantern, leads Christine by her hand as the travelator slowly tilts downward and they make their way through the Labyrinth Underground to the boat that takes them across the misty waters to the Phantom's lair. Finally, when the journey by boat to the lair was tweaked to perfection, we knew it would be another magical element of the show.

Phantom, as it is known in the theatrical world, opened at Her Majesty's Theatre on October 9, 1986, to a prolonged standing ovation. It is now a phenomenon. It became the longest running musical on Broadway, closing in 2023. It is today the second-longest running show in London's West End, the first being Cameron Mackintosh's *Les Misérables*. Hal's words that "the audience must experience a sense of an occasion" were certainly true.

The Princess visited the show both officially and unofficially. She loved the romance and spectacle of it and appreciated the production that much more for hearing a fair number of behind-the-scenes moments from me. One of her favourite songs was "All I Ask of You," which the series *The Crown* portrayed Diana singing.

CHAPTER SIXTEEN

A Reception, a Realization, and a Resolution

I T WAS HARD TO believe that we were heading towards the end of another year, making it five years since Diana and I had our first meeting. We had managed to keep our classes private, even though there were now a few more people who knew it was happening, but no one outside those few had discovered where the classes took place or who was there or what went on. The main thing was that the press did not get wind of them, and we could continue.

In early December, I was delighted when my husband and I received an invitation to a reception to be held in the State Apartments at Kensington Palace on Thursday, December 11, 1986, at 6 p.m. The "Christmas Do"!

To go to Kensington Palace at Christmas was both an honour and a thrilling surprise. A select group of close friends and people who important in both Charles and Diana's lives were invited, but not quite as many as had been invited to garden parties. This was a more intimate gathering of a few hundred as opposed to a few thousand. Christmas is a very special time of the year and what could be better than to visit a palace, even if the exterior of Kensington Palace is not what is imagined when thinking of palaces.

It was originally built as a house in 1605 and was bought in 1689 to become the home of King William III and Queen Mary II. It was transformed from a mansion into a palace by the famous architect Sir Christopher Wren, renowned for designing St. Paul's Cathedral, where Charles and Diana were wed. Queen Victoria spent her childhood at Kensington Palace and it is where she became a monarch in 1837. Over the years, the palace has gone through many major refurbishments and expansions. It was severely damaged during the Second World War, but since then has been restored to grandeur with a new entrance and exquisite gardens. It was the royal residence for Charles and Diana after their marriage.

My husband and I decided to take a private car that evening, which was a treat. We were dropped inside the gates of Kensington Palace, right at the entrance door for the reception. The chauffeur opened the doors of the car for us, which made us feel very special. As we entered, we were dazzled by the splendor of the King's Staircase and walked very slowly up each step, taking in its beauty with magnificent Italian paintings on the walls and on the ceiling. I almost felt I could hear the walls whispering stories about those people from the past.

As we entered the reception room, the richness of the red walls, adorned by more artwork, created a beautiful ambience. We were walking on air, our happy hearts full as we were invited to sip champagne and toast one another on this memorable evening. Wayne had also been invited. Amidst a very busy room decked with Christmas glitter, we managed to connect. We were all quite giddy with excitement and, perhaps, the bubbles of the champagne.

Elizabeth and David Emanuel came over to say hello, which was lovely, as I had only met them once or twice before when they had designed a costume for Wayne. They were warm and friendly, and I laughed to myself remembering the day I had watched the fairytale wedding dress make its entrance, as Lady Diana stepped out of the carriage, the train drifting behind her as she walked into St. Paul's to become the Princess of Wales. The Emanuels would always be known for that dress. They also had designed outfits for the Princess's recent trip to Saudi Arabia, which showed how sensitive and tasteful they were with respect to the culture. Their black-and-white silk satin gown, which featured a striped bow, was a big success. In addition, they had designed a full-length abaya that was packed as a reserve outfit and which had been made at the request of Diana's staff, in case something more modest and conservative was needed.

Catherine Walker was another beautiful designer in attendance and she, too, made a point of coming over to say hello. I was pleased that she knew my name! I was in awe of her elegant, sophisticated designs, and matching personality. I knew the Princess admired her and loved her work. I was happy to think that maybe Diana had told her about our dance classes (and very sad to hear of Catherine's passing in 2010).

Anne Beckwith-Smith came by and took us over to say hello to Diana and Charles. Anne was masterful in how she handled everything. Always putting everyone at their ease and taking care to monitor any difficulties that might occur. Diana greeted us warmly, and Charles was lovely, too. They appeared to be happy, or at least had learned to put on a united front; it seemed everyone was in the spirit of Christmas. Wayne joined us and, as always, he made the Princess laugh. He had met Charles a few times before, so there were some fun exchanges between them. After that, we politely stepped away.

Knowing the protocol of stepping away at the appropriate moment was encouraged by Anne. There were always so many people the royal couple had to greet that Anne would tactfully encourage guests to say hello and not linger. Wayne was chatting on a bit, so Anne gently ushered him away.

After about an hour of pure bliss, Anne made her way back to me, pulling me gently to one side. She asked if I could please do something about Wayne as, in her words, he was continuing to bother the Princess when she had duties to attend. Wayne loved to have a bit of fun and I presumed that maybe he had consumed one too many glasses of champagne. The Princess genuinely did very much enjoy his company. I thought it best for all if I spoke to Wayne, and told Anne I would find him. She was grateful, as she did not want security to step in. This comment took me aback. It felt extreme, but I presumed they were just being protective.

When I did get to Wayne, I could see the louder side of him coming out, even if he was genuinely just having a good time. His behaviour was inappropriate for this inner royal circle. I managed to placate the situation and draw him away. I knew, too, that he was aware of what was being done.

The incident burst my bubble of elation, but as the evening was soon ending, I tried not to let it bother me too much. We sailed back down the King's Staircase on the way out, treasuring the experience.

Over the next few days, I was a bit troubled by having been asked to deal with the incident with Wayne and wondered why Anne felt it necessary to do so. Perhaps she was just doing what had been asked of her.

There now had been a couple of instances outside the sanctity of our dance studio where I had sensed the amount of pressure that Diana was under in fulfilling her role as Princess of Wales. I had seen first-hand how everything Diana did had to be met with approval in the eyes of the monarchy, and this expectation seemed to be enforced by the working entourage that surrounded her. I'm sure there were instances where protection was required, but I couldn't help feeling that having her under constant watch was more what "they" wanted than what Diana wanted.

Wayne had proved to be a very trustworthy friend to the Princess, and she enjoyed his company, but I don't think their friendship was met with approval. It appeared to me that being too close to anyone who was not within the royal circle was not encouraged. This realization was another tiny lesson for me.

My thoughts about the pressure Diana was under to conform to "their" requirements were clarified at our next class. Wayne and I had invited Diana to lunch, which we had scheduled for the following week. When we were in the studio, Diana told me, with a laugh in her voice, that she was very much looking forward to having lunch with us, even though "they" had tried to reschedule something for that day.

In making the decision to come to lunch when it would have been easy for her to give us an excuse was another example of Diana strengthening her resolve to assert a little more of herself. This event was certainly not in the Princess's official diary, but she was going to honour it because there were friendships that she wanted to keep for herself. At that instance, I saw a tiny bit of a rebel princess who wasn't always going to be dictated to:

> *Thank you so much for taking me out to lunch on Monday. . . . I do hope that we will be able to do it again. . . . What pleasure it brought to this particular lady [smiley face].*

Another highlight of that Christmas season was a card received by my two daughters, Emily and Victoria, signed by all the royal family.

CHAPTER SEVENTEEN

Breaking Barriers

I T WAS 1987. The beginning of the new year brought a stronger Princess of Wales, who was starting to define "who she was in that role," as she put it. She had discovered the things that really mattered to her and realized that she could make a difference by bringing attention to them as the Princess of Wales. She began to let herself show and feel sensitivity and empathy to those who were in distress or suffering. She was widening her knowledge and understanding from what she now considered her sheltered upbringing. She knew her position as Princess of Wales would never allow her to see the world as it really was, so she made the decision to raise awareness about those less fortunate than herself, whenever or wherever she could. She was resolute that being more confident in herself might give her the ability to improve and change people's lives. As she spoke of this during one of our after-class floor chats, I could see the truth in her eyes and the deep sense of purpose that she felt.

I think it is extremely hard for people to take in what Diana's diary looked like and what she fit into her day. Most started with a morning swim, and was then jam-packed with appointments, making sure every charity got the right attention, and followed by public appearances that went on into the evening. Diana was very much in demand.

Now that she had found her purpose, which was crucial to her, she did everything she could to bring the right attention to every person she met. She had already abandoned certain protocols: usually she didn't wear gloves so she could shake hands with people that needed to feel a human touch, and often didn't wear hats if the engagement involved her meeting children because it was easier to hug them. Her natural way of chatting and genuinely enjoying the conversation made her much more accessible than any royal before her. Diana thought it was desperately important that the monarchy have closer contact with its people, and the public loved her for that.

In her private life, she wanted Charles to see what she was capable of, and for him to be proud of her. Although she was still upset about the knowledge that Charles was seeing Camilla, she hoped things would change. One of her biggest concerns was that her children did not suffer; their well-being was the most important thing on her mind. She loved more than anything being a mum and, when she could, she would take her boys to school and spend as much time with them as her schedule would permit. More than anything, she wanted the boys to be allowed to connect with the world outside the palace. She wanted them to experience all walks of life and felt it was most important that they understand other people's emotions. "The royal way" was the opposite of that. She was determined that they would have a deeper understanding of people, which ultimately would serve them in their future lives.

Her growing confidence showed in her physical appearance too. It had become easier for her to lift her head and carry herself more assuredly. She made brave and bold choices in the outfits she wore, reflecting a renewed strength. For example, when she greeted King Fahd of Saudi

Arabia on his visit to Britain in March, she wore a stunning cream suit designed by Catherine Walker. Almost military in style, it gave the sense that she was expressing a command of herself, but still with elegance. Earlier that March, she had chosen a tuxedo to wear to a jazz ballet performance at the Hippodrome night club in London, where she was met by its owner, Peter Stringfellow. The outfit showed both the masculine power and the feminine flair of her character. She had worn tuxedo style before, but this one came off with gallant elegance.

Peter Stringfellow had changed the old cabaret-style club known as Talk of the Town to the Hippodrome to create the "world's greatest disco." The year before, he had opened a successful night club called Stringfellows in New York, which lots of celebrities frequented. It was seen as risky that a a member of the royal family would attend a night club. Diana, of course. was most interested in seeing the dancing. She laughed one day as she said to me, "It does have its perks too, being the Princess of Wales. I get good seats at the theatre and get to see the latest James Bond or Superman movie premieres."

But the moment that truly defined Diana came in April of that year. It was a miraculous, spontaneous moment that would give the world an unforgettable image of her. I believe it showed the quintessence of the woman she really was. And it all came about from the simple gesture of a handshake with a young man suffering from HIV/AIDS.

HIV/AIDS first came to the attention of the medical community in 1981. The next year, after Terrence Higgins was one of the first to die from the AIDS virus in the U.K., his friends set up the Terrence Higgins Trust to increase awareness about the virus and to prevent its spread. (Princess Margaret became its patron.)

In Scotland, the Scottish AIDS Monitor was set up by Derek Ogg in 1983 to educate gay men about the risks of HIV and AIDS. Derek had read about the spread of the disease in the United States and knew it would travel fast. The British government finally launched prevention activities in 1986, including a campaign with the slogan "AIDS: Don't Die of Ignorance." With that finally came the necessary research to help combat the illness.

In April 1987, Diana had been invited to open the HIV/AIDS unit at the Middlesex Hospital in London, a facility that would focus exclusively on the care of patients with the disease. She had done a great deal of research before her visit. She felt she was hampered by her ignorance and wanted to be more knowledgeable. She had talked to specialist doctors on the subject in order to fully understand the difficulties that HIV-positive patients faced. Their pain was greater than any fear she felt of the consequences she might experience for doing something that was not considered a fitting choice for the Princess of Wales. She wanted to be taken more seriously and to be recognized as doing more than shaking dignitaries' hands, planting trees, cutting ribbons, and being noticed for what she wore. And so, when she entered the ward, she reached out with her ungloved hand and shook the hand of a young man with HIV/AIDS. It was this gesture that helped dispel the widespread myth that HIV/AIDS could spread by touch.

Although there were many who fought over the years to bring the right information and knowledge to the public, it was this instinctive gesture from Diana that paved the way to dispel the social stigma that came with the disease. In that instant, Diana spontaneously took the hand of the patient to show she cared and that he was not alone, and helped us understand the great need for human connection in the care of those suffering with HIV/AIDS.

Diana was discovering her inner power. She was coming to understand that she could be effective in changing and improving people's lives, and she would show no boundaries when raising awareness for causes that mattered to her. She had broken through a barrier for herself.

CHAPTER EIGHTEEN

Another Bump!

T WAS TOWARD the end of May when, to my utter surprise, I discovered I was pregnant.

I had done a test at the doctor's and then had gone shopping at Harrods as a complete distraction, awaiting the result. Pregnancy home tests were available, but not trusted for their reliability. I sat having a coffee and cake in the café at Harrods before phoning the doctor's office. I was gobsmacked, but thrilled. I walked about looking at things I couldn't afford, trying to get my head together. Three children! My husband was delighted when I told him the news that evening, but we both did feel a bit of panic.

We were now living in a flat we had bought in 1984, having had to leave our rented Highgate haven because the owner was selling the house in which the girls shared a bedroom. This apartment would not accommodate two adults and three children. We would have to move. That was the first problem. The next problem was that Hal Prince and Gillian Lynne had asked me to go to New York with the artistic team to mount the upcoming production of *The Phantom of the Opera*, which was due to open on Broadway in January 1988.

The idea of working on Broadway was exciting, of course, but I would be over seven months pregnant by the time rehearsals would start and, by then, I would probably be advised not to fly. In addition, a vast bump would not be conducive to demonstrating ballet moves. To top it off, the baby was due just before Christmas, at the height of the most crucial time: on-stage rehearsals.

I felt a real sense of duty to my work with Gillian. I had been looking after her artistic work on the show on a weekly basis, going to three or four performances a week, and running the rehearsals. This allowed me to keep her and Hal up to date with the critical details that were so vital in making sure the standard of the performance never slipped, by giving notes to actors or rehearsing choreography and scenes that needed to be tightened up.

I was uniquely positioned to do this because I had been allowed to witness what was in Gillian's head as she created the scenes and the choreography, and I had kept copious notes. I could recreate exactly what she had done, with all her dramatic intention, and that's what she would need for Broadway. The other key players on the team were the production stage manager, who took care of everything technical as well as the well-being of the actors, and the music director, who took care of everything vocal.

Maintaining a show is a relentless process. The working week for performers includes eight shows (two days had both a matinee and an evening performance). Understudy rehearsals start immediately after opening night. Usually there are two rehearsal days, of four to five hours each, for understudies or maintenance. It can be gruelling. Fortunately, there is an Actors Equity ruling that an actor cannot work on their day off or the following day until the evening performance. This allows much-needed rest, for both the vocal cords and the body.

The purpose of the rehearsals is to have understudies ready to go should anything happen to an actor, either through illness or injury. The understudies will have begun studying the rehearsal process by watching, but now they must learn the stagecraft and details of how the lead actor plays the role. The intention of the understudy is to precisely recreate what that actor does on stage. This way, the audience will not be aware that there is a change, except by reading the understudy's name in a program insert. In the case of *Phantom*, people came to see Michael Crawford, but there had to be an understudy of the highest calibre should anything unforeseen happen to him.

The importance of these on-stage rehearsals is also for the safety of the actor when the set is moving. The actor must be cognizant of the timing of large moving set pieces, as well as other actors running on and off stage—to know the timing and the *traffic* backstage, as we call it.

Gillian had been working closely with Michael Crawford, coaching him as he delved into uncovering every aspect of the Phantom, and I was lucky to be always privy to her private rehearsals with him. Michael was always respectful when receiving feedback from me, should it need to be given, which was hardly ever. He was a perfectionist and knew the importance of each performance, because each member of each audience was different, and he wanted them all to live the experience the first time they saw the show. In *Phantom*'s case, many patrons saw the show multiple times.

Performing eight shows a week over many months can alter an actor's work, because of the repetition. Keeping the performance spontaneous and in the moment is the biggest challenge for actors in long-term contracts. Most actors are grateful for the input of notes from outside observers, from the perspective of the audience, and the resident director, which I was also acting as. It was their chance to make improvements.

Again, I really wanted to stay involved with *Phantom*, but I knew I would have to tell Hal and Gillian that I couldn't do it. It was in everyone's best interest. Since we were months away, I would make sure that I could pass all the information and notes I had to the person who would be taking over from me in assisting Gillian.

I was a little worried about breaking my news to Diana. This development would mean I'd be away from the dance classes for a few weeks before and after the birth. I also felt that it was important to be there for her, should she need to talk. Our conversations had become more and more frequent and often revolved around the difficult position she found herself in with her husband.

Diana had just come back from an official visit to the 40th International Cannes Film Festival, where she stunned onlookers in her romantic light-blue, tulle, floaty gown designed by Catherine Walker. It was very reminiscent of the dress the late Princess Grace had worn when she was an actress. Diana and Charles were there to represent Britain and to honour British films. Diana's very presence did much to boost business for Britain, a fact that tends to be overlooked and underappreciated. Although she had learned that she could make a difference with her support, she was often unaware of the profound impact that she had with any personal appearance. Diana was more in awe of the film stars that she admired, never appreciating that she, too, shone brightly.

As I watched television footage of the festival and caught glimpses of her, I felt there was a definite distance between the couple. I told myself that maybe I was reading too much into appearances. There had also been the devastating news at the beginning of the trip that Brian Mannakee, a former detective that Diana was very fond of, had been killed in a motorcycle accident. The circumstances of his death disturbed Diana.

When I asked Diana, at our next class, how she was doing, her face said it all. She had been devastated by Brian's death. She then turned immediately to ongoing problems with Charles. "We manage to put on a good official front, but it's getting more and more difficult, as I find it very hard not to show how I feel if I am upset. Charles seems to want us to lead separate lives. Anne, he runs off to Camilla whenever he can. It's not at all what I want. I'd like the marriage to work, but it just isn't for now. Do I just put up with it, hoping he will change?"

I was very troubled for her. I could feel her anguish. Because Diana had shared with me her private feelings, I felt I could ask her what she thought she could do and if she felt living separate lives was a situation she could endure. She listened intently, then wanted to discuss what that would mean, so I asked if she could see herself not having any romance, affection, or love in her life? She smiled coyly. "All I want is to be with Charles and be loved by him, there's just emptiness just now," she told me. I decided to be brave, asking if she could live without love and what about sex in her life? She blushed, but was delighted I had raised this very personal question. She admitted that these were all things she had been considering and felt tremendous relief to be able to talk with me about them.

It was then that Diana told me she had met someone who made her feel much better about herself. My instant reaction was delight for her. "It's just wonderful to be with someone that cares about me," she said. She knew she could talk freely, and the conversations would not be discussed outside the room we were in. I respected the privacy of our conversation. It made me happy to know that someone was caring for her in an affectionate, loving way, even though I was concerned that it might cause her hurt if it became known.

When I told Diana at the end of the class of my pregnancy, she seemed a little taken aback. I assured her it would not interfere with our classes, although she would be having to look at a big bump in a few months, and I certainly did not want my well-being to worry her.

It occurred to me, in that instant, that maybe she might want more children. She was only twenty-six, but she told me that that was probably unlikely, given the situation. Her comment made me a little sad, knowing she still had so much time ahead of her.

Ever gracious, she sent me a lovely letter congratulating me on my pregnancy, which I received the next day:

This comes with a huge round of applause . . . & much love as always,
Diana

CHAPTER NINETEEN

Unloading

OR DIANA, BEING able to unload some of her personal problems allowed her to regain her focus and enjoy our dancing classes as the weeks went on. Although things were not resolved in her marriage, she had given herself permission to enjoy a little bit of a private life, but knew in her heart that it was not the solution. There were moments when Charles and Diana were seen together where there did appear to be affection between them. One such occasion, when she presented him with a trophy after he won a polo match, was delightful.

By late summer, in time for the new term of school. I had moved to Sunninghill, which is very near Windsor. My husband had been offered a job there, and we had managed to find a house we could afford with enough rooms to accommodate our growing family.

Diana, always kind, and showing her sense of humour, sent me a card for my new home. It was a cartoon of a castle with the Union Jack flying and a woman saying to a man, "It's not much but we like to call it home."

Our new address meant a commute of an hour to Waterloo by train, which involved an early start on the days of classes with Diana. It was worth it to me. In fact, once I had flown from Aberdeen to London just to make our class, and then returned to Aberdeen just in time for a performance. This I had kept to myself.

The weeks and months seemed to fly by. I was now eight months pregnant. One day in November, my husband came with the girls to pick me up after my class with Diana. We were going to have an outing in London together, before the baby was born. Diana and I would have just a few more classes before I stopped for the year. And probably a good thing, as it had been a taxing journey getting to the studio that morning.

From the minute the class started, I could tell Diana was distracted and troubled. She tried very hard to work through her feelings, but I could see from her body language and her fatigue after a short routine that this was not something she could throw off. She was dealing with feelings and emotions very deep inside her, and I knew she wanted to express them, but it was very difficult—she felt so vulnerable. In pure despair, she dropped to the floor, sobbing. I was distressed for her. I could feel the pain and turmoil she was in. I let her just cry.

After a few minutes, apologizing profusely for dumping on me when I had enough on my mind, she started to talk through the tears. "I just don't know what to do, Anne. I find myself in an unbearable situation. I haven't seen Charles for weeks and he doesn't want to talk to me. I thought he would come back to me, and we could work things out. How do I go on when I'm not wanted?" Her hurt was deep, and she could not see a way through it. My heart was broken for her.

I can still vividly remember the deep anxiety and dread she felt, the emotional conflict within her, and her fear for the future. It was a complex situation and she was searching for honest answers and solutions. The question of separation had been brought up, but I didn't believe that separation was an option, and told her. The palace would never agree, and I honestly didn't think that was what she wanted. Diana wanted Charles to be with her and to love her. Even though she was in her own romantic affair, at this point, Charles was still the man she desired and that was why it was so agonizing for her. "Keeping my family together is the most important thing to me," she said, still crying.

When the detective knocked on the studio door, we both realized we were way over time. The Princess shouted, "Coming!" She picked herself up, pulled herself together, and headed off to change.

Once she had spent a few minutes in the dressing room, her demeanour brightened, and she told me she felt heaps better after talking. I knew she was putting on a brave front. "Let's say hello to the girls," she said. As ever, her warmth with children was beautiful, Emily, now aged ten, sweetly asked how William and Harry were, and Diana told Emily that they couldn't wait for Christmas. Victoria, just two years old, held her sister's hand and smiled at Diana when she bent down beside her. I doubt that the girls remember the meeting, but I would never forget it.

That evening, even though it had been a fun afternoon visiting the Hamleys toy shop in London, I took myself out for a private walk after the girls had gone to bed. My husband thought it was just pregnancy rituals, but the truth was, I had been very affected by the morning with Diana and was still trying to process the information she had given me. Yes, there had been strong indications before, but there was something in this conversation that really troubled me, and it wasn't pregnancy hormones that were making me overreact. It was the big crack in her marriage that had not yet broken apart but had the potential to do so.

Diana was terrified that the press would find out the seriousness of her marital situation, and the potential harm and damage that such a revelation could have on her children. It was overwhelming for her, and not without foundation as rumours of their troubled marriage had been swirling in the tabloid press over the last few months.

Since her engagement and fairytale wedding six years earlier, Diana had captivated the press. The competition was fierce among the papers and, because the reporters knew that any news of her would sell copies, they would go to any length, and pay any amount, to get a story or a shot. They often used binoculars or long-lens cameras, not caring one bit about the privacy of the individual or the potential harm they could do. Unfortunately, the majority of people would believe what was written in a newspaper. Scruples were out the window.

Around that time, Diana told me that she was being followed every time she left her home because the press had realized that she and Charles were not spending much time together. Charles had gone to Balmoral, while Diana stayed in London with the children. That was true, but what the situation told me was that reporters were paying an inordinate amount of attention to their private lives, as opposed to their public roles. Imagine trying to live with public reactions as your life played out in the media. The pressure on her was tremendous.

I also felt the pressure. I could not share any of these confidences that she had shared with me with anyone. I wanted to be a good friend and give advice if asked, and yet I wasn't qualified to understand the complexities of her position. All I could do was listen and offer support until a light was shed on what was needed to be done. I felt a little relief when a letter arrived for me the next day:

You were so marvelous to me today as I loaded my problems onto your shoulders. Thank you, Anne, for caring and being an extraordinary special friend.

CHAPTER TWENTY

Just Keep Going

DIANA AND I completed our dancing classes in early December. The following weeks found me deep in my nesting instinct, but my mind kept thinking about her and if she was doing all right. I was concerned about her mental well-being. It was amazing to me that, no matter how she was feeling personally, she did not let it show when she attended her engagements. Her work was far too important to her and gave her great solace.

On her visit to Glasgow in early December, she visited the Possilpark Drugs Project, where she met young addicts in recovery. The press photos caught her deep concern and sympathy as she listened to their difficult stories. In this area of the city, there was much unemployment and hardship, which could account for the high number of drug users. It was very much in keeping with Diana's values that she wanted to spend at least a bit of time helping others if she could, even if just to say a few kind words. In return, the public offered her great admiration, and even that, I believe, could be a bit overwhelming for her at times.

A few days later, she was in the news again, this time at the Great

Ormond Street Hospital in London, where she helped Santa give out early Christmas presents to the children, who beamed at her. She topped Santa that day!

I wanted to let her know that I was thinking of her and knew the annual Friends Gala at the Opera House was coming up. Diana had wanted to *dance* again in performance, but knew that wasn't a possibility. I decided, spontaneously, that I would send her flowers just to say, "Thinking of you." She sent a beautiful letter back, which made me feel that she had very much appreciated the gesture:

> *You are a complete wonder to have sent me the flowers and v touching note with them . . . leaves me speechless (& that's quite an achievement!) I am about to go off to the opera house, feeling quite empty at the prospect of not being able to do my dance.*

I knew that if the baby hadn't popped out by then, I would be seeing Diana at the Kensington Palace Christmas reception, to which my husband and I had been invited again. As it turned out, I was in luck and was able to attend. I hoped that our going would take my mind off the waiting.

Being in the beautiful surroundings of Kensington Palace again was something I could never be blasé about. I pinched myself each time. The wonderful thing about being nine months pregnant is that everyone around you is kind, giving you space, offering you seats, and treating you with such consideration.

The Princess hugged me warmly, as we both laughed at the bump in the way. She was so sympathetic and understood from her own experience how difficult it can be when you sail by your due date. She made me promise that I would immediately let her know when the baby finally made an entrance.

Receiving the Christmas card that year brought me renewed faith that things were better in her marriage. The card was signed *Diana and Charles*, and it certainly was a well-chosen happy family image. It seemed as though Diana had decided to just keep going, and I sincerely hoped that their situation was improving.

CHAPTER TWENTY-ONE

Welcome to the Boys' Team

"WELCOME TO THE boys' team" was the note on the card Diana sent for me, along with a beautiful bouquet of flowers, on December 22, 1987. Alastair Peter Allan had been born at 1:32 p.m. on the day before. It was a thrill to have a son and a total surprise, as I felt sure that I would have another girl. Dad was filled with pride at having a boy. My Scottish family were also delighted—it was the first boy in years. The girls immediately took care of their little brother and smothered him with love.

Having the baby a few days before Christmas was not the most ideal situation, as there were still the last-minute errands to be done. I trudged out of bed to go to Windsor on December 23 to shop for a few hours. Even that was a big mistake. By the time I returned home, I was glad to lie flat for a few days, awaiting the arrival of my darling mum who flew to my rescue from Glasgow. She was eager to check out her new grandson.

The Princess spent Christmas at Windsor Castle; ironically, she was just down the road from me, as Sunninghill was approximately seven miles away. Windsor Castle is the oldest occupied castle in the world, dating back to the days of William the Conqueror in the eleventh century, the oldest part being the motte on which the Round Tower stands. It has been updated throughout the centuries with both Georgian and Victorian designs, and with Gothic features reinvented in a more modern style. It proudly stands in the centre of the town of Windsor, where William Shakespeare is said to have written *The Merry Wives of Windsor* at what is now the Ye Olde King's Head pub. You can walk down the cobbled streets of the town to the castle, stand right next it, and touch the stone walls. You can feel and sense its history. That it is still occupied is a wonder. The stone walls make it difficult to heat the interior, which is why large tapestries are hung on the walls and there are three hundred massive fireplaces. Nonetheless, Diana told me, "It's *still* very cold in there!"

The Great Park that surrounds the castle is a magnificent sight, extending for miles with the Long Walk that leads right up to the castle gates. People stroll by, looking up to check whether the Royal Standard is flying. If the flag is flying, the monarch is at home. Up until 2022, it was Queen Elizabeth II. Today, it is King Charles III.

I had enjoyed seeing the television clips of the royal family coming out of St. George's Chapel on Christmas Day as I sat in my home, still in my PJs, with my feet up. Diana looked like she was having a lot of fun with the children, which made me happy. It was also a joy to see William, age five, attending the service for the first time. St. George's Chapel is a place of many royal celebrations, and a mausoleum for many monarchs. It is where the late Queen Elizabeth II was laid to rest.

Diana had made a comment in her letter—"I'm thinking of you a lot and smiling every time I realize that you are a mother of three!" This new reality, and the complexities it brought, suddenly hit me. I first was taking my son, at six weeks old, to Glasgow to have the family Scottish

Blessing. My husband was not able to travel with me but would join us in a couple of days.

Getting everyone on the plane was a challenge. Victoria, who was just over two, needed to hold my hand, and have my attention, while I carried Alastair in my other arm and checked that Emily, who now didn't have a hand to hold, was still right beside me. It was worth it to uphold our tradition of wetting the baby's head and lips with a fine malt whisky to bless him, and putting a piece of silver in his tiny hand to see if he would hold on to it. If he did, it would declare that he was going to be wealthy! If he didn't, it would declare that he was going to be poor! They were ridiculous but fun customs, and really an excuse to toast the newborn with a lot of Scotch. Baby Alastair passed the test and was suitably passed around the family to have a "wee hold." Fortunately, he was a very placid baby.

Before I had left for Glasgow, it had been confirmed that I would travel to Vienna the second week of January 1988 to attend auditions for *The Phantom of the Opera* (*Das Phantom der Oper*), which was scheduled to open there in December 1989. I had agreed to go because there was no one else available who knew the show. The original team was in New York City, preparing the Broadway production that was due to open on January 20. I had thought, rather stupidly, that the baby would make its entrance much earlier than he did, and I would be fine and recovered in time to go. Well, "the best laid schemes o'mice an' men gang aft agley," meaning no matter the planning, things can still go wrong. Alastair's birth was two weeks late. I had just a couple of weeks to get my strength back and get into dancing mode. I would need to demonstrate the ballet combinations at the auditions. It was only going to be three days, I told myself, so it could be done!

I should have guessed that, if I was flying to Vienna for *Phantom* auditions only three weeks after the birth of my son, the new year was going to be a bumpy ride. There was something wonderful about not knowing it at the time. I managed to get through the auditions, although my body was not happy, a good reminder to myself about how important it was to allow myself to heal correctly and build muscle strength over time.

Once back home, I was notified that I would resume classes with Diana in February. The Princess was scheduled to have a tour to Australia to celebrate its bicentenary in late January. Meanwhile, I would have a few weeks to continue my recovery.

CHAPTER TWENTY-TWO

The Value of Time

I ENJOYED THE TREASURED time with my new son and family while the Princess was away on her ten-day, action-packed tour to Australia.

There may have been additional pressure on her during this time as rumours were constantly hitting the British tabloids regarding the young couple's marriage. There was no evidence of any discord on the trip, as the Princess was radiant as always, and shined in the public eye. The Australian press lapped it up. I thought to myself, *how many hands does she or any royal shake in a day and how many in a year?* It must be an incredible number.

The itinerary on their tour included: a ride on a steam train and paddle boat; a spectacular fashion show at the iconic Sydney Opera House that managed to bring some of the world's biggest designers together; a surfing carnival, where Diana stood blushing amidst a line of lifeguards in their tight Speedos, cameras snapping madly as she laughed and joked; a royal concert at which Olivia Newton-John and John Denver performed; official dinners; walkabouts in the scorching heat; and an impromptu piano-playing moment by Diana at a music college in Melbourne, which she carried out even though her vulnerability was evident—she almost ran away with embarrassment at the delightful response it brought.

The bicentennial Australian tour had been tremendously successful. Charles and Diana then travelled to Thailand, where she continued to glow. The tour did much to convince the public that things seemed to be fine between the royal couple. I was looking forward to seeing her to find out for myself.

Diana and Charles arrived home at the beginning of February. For our first class, the door of the dance studio flew open and Diana danced in. I was so glad to see her and to see how lively she was. Hugging me warmly, she immediately inquired, "How is it being a mum of three?" She handed me a present of the most delicate fine wool cardigans for Alastair, such a special and thoughtful gift. "It's still very cold and he will need them," she said.

The tour had been exhausting for her, but she had enjoyed it and had thrown herself into the work, trying to put her difficulties aside, because "that was far more important," she said.

After a few minutes of chatting, we went to the ballet barre and started as we always did, facing each other, now with her able to connect eye to eye as we went through our warm-up. By this time, the movements were so engrained in her muscle memory that I was able to watch and correct her positioning, as needed. She smiled as she came back to the basics of dance.

In ballet, we always begin at the start—pliés, battement tendu, battement glissé, grand battement, adagio, and so on. Our warm-up was both in ballet and jazz forms. There are similarities in the techniques, although jazz is freer, but both require excellent balance. Knowing each movement and repeating them as you warm up brings a security to your body. Your muscles don't fight the movement once you get to know it. Diana content-edly brought her focus to the moment. We kept that mood as we moved through the class. Instead of talking, we just danced, and let the language of dance speak for itself.

The next few weeks continued happily in the same way. Then disaster hit.

Diana was pale and drawn when we met for our class. It was shortly after the horrendous accident that took place on March 10, 1988. She and Charles had been on their skiing break to Klosters, in the Swiss Alps. A very close friend, Major Hugh Lindsay, had been killed in an avalanche while skiing with Charles. Another friend, Patti Palmer-Tomkinson, suffered serious leg injuries. Diana sat down to tell me all this, tears filling her eyes.

It had been the longest wait of her life, she said, to have to sit in the chalet after the initial phone call that let her know there had been a serious accident and to wait for more news. She did not know who was hurt, or whether it might be Charles. The next call brought the distressing news that Major Lindsay, only thirty-four years old and close to both Diana and Charles, had died. Her heart was heavy as she told me that his wife, Sarah, had remained at home in England, skipping the trip because she was seven months pregnant with their first child. Charles, miraculously, was not hurt, but the shock that he might have been dead was too much for Diana to bear.

When Charles had finally arrived back at the chalet, she could see the tremendous shock he was in. She had to stay calm. She knew what had to be done and organized their return trip for the next day. Charles had been resistant, but she knew she was right, and understood the trauma he was in. The party returned home, travelling in silence. When they were back in London, she immediately went to be with Sarah.

The funeral had been difficult to get through, and the aftermath of the tragedy had left Diana with deep feelings of grief. She vowed to herself to value time and not dwell on the futility of conflicts, particularly petty rows. She would try to break from the past and take to heart the lessons of the tragedy.

I could see over the next few weeks that a heaviness continued to weigh on the Princess. She expressed that there seemed to be a closeness with her husband for a short while, but it was fleeting. During our next class, she mentioned she felt as though things were caving in and it was causing her distress. Diana could not do any dancing; instead, an outpouring of feelings flooded out. I knew she was at her lowest ebb.

This letter came the next day, where she expressed that sharing her troubles made her feel a lot better:

> *I felt heaps better talking about it. On return I had a good blub and spent the rest of the morning in my bed—I'm ashamed to admit. I appreciated your patience and understanding . . . & I got strength from your wisdom and kindness.*

CHAPTER TWENTY-THREE

The Epiphany

EXT CAME THE phone call from Anne-Beckwith Smith at the palace. "The Princess may want to stop her dance classes and do something else," she told me. I was taken aback. I'd always known that something like this might happen, that the Princess might want to make a change. Still, I found it very surprising. In fact, I was astounded. I found myself saying through my shock, "Oh, of course, if that's what she would like." Anne Beckwith-Smith continued, "I will let you know when, of course, and we want to tell you how much we appreciate your time with Her Royal Highness." I put the phone down, stunned, and sat in a daze for the next few minutes.

I went through the day and was glad I was at home where I could just focus on my children. I tried not to think too much, but it was exceptionally difficult. I was confused and tried to work through the logic of what I had heard. My first thoughts were that maybe Diana was looking for some other form of exercise.

We were in the 1980s and the gym era was starting. There had always been different forms of workouts over the years, but this was the beginning of something new, something we now accept as the norm, *going to the gym*. Fitness centres and Nautilus Studios had started to emerge, and along with them came the rise of the boutique gym.

Even I had started to go to body conditioning classes, which today would be called Pilates. I did find it incredibly strengthening and wished we had been introduced to it during my years of training as a classical dancer. Pilates strengthens the body by focusing on therapeutic training of specific muscles and on increasing core connection, which can do a lot to avoid injury. It is now used worldwide and has been a large component in raising the standard of technique for many dancers. Today, there is so much more knowledge about fitness and training that can help you become the best dancer possible.

I wondered if maybe this might be something Diana would like to try, or perhaps her friends were attending gyms and she wanted to experience it, too. I also considered whether it had become more difficult for her to make time for dancing, as she had become more focused on her work.

Then there's the moment one's ego spurs the inner monologue of doubt: maybe what I was doing was not what she wanted, and she found it difficult to tell me, in case I felt hurt. I knew that the classes would stop one day and our time would be over. Was this it? I would be sad, yes, but I had a lot I would cherish. I wasn't sure the best way to handle the situation or even if I should ask Diana directly. I would trust my instincts and knew that the right approach would come to me.

At the next class a few days later, Diana and I did our warm-up and were moving on to do our centre work when, without any expectation, I decided to say that I had been told that she might like to stop her classes and would be happy to offer any information that she might need if she wanted to experience something else. Diana looked at me, completely blank. "What are you talking about?" she asked. I explained the phone call from Anne Beckwith-Smith. I could tell Diana was annoyed, as she told me categorically that was not the case: she loved the classes and valued our time together. At the end of the class, she reassured me there would be a next one.

I went for a walk after class and it hit me. It wasn't Diana who wanted to stop the classes. It was the Palace who wanted her to stop. In our private classes there were just the two of us in the room, so no one ever knew what was said between us. The detectives, who were outside, could probably hear music when we were dancing, but there were many classes when we just chatted. Yet I knew the detectives were always supportive of Diana and I could see how much she enjoyed their company—I knew they were on her side.

If it was the Palace, or the "establishment," that wanted her to stop the classes, what were they worried about? Did they worry that I might have information about the Princess's marriage that they did not want to be shared? Did they really think I was the kind of person that would tell other people? Did they really think I would go to the press—was that their fear? Were they just being protective? Or did they really want that much control over her own private time? These questions made me uncomfortable, but I knew I was right in thinking them.

I further concluded that the "establishment" may not have been happy about the subject Diana had shared with me a few classes before, when she couldn't do any dancing. Instead, she had crumbled into a heap, telling me she had something to confess. It was such a strong word, *confess,* that it instantly alarmed me. What on earth could be so bad that was causing her such torment? I assured her that there was nothing that would shock me and that a worry shared would take the weight out of it.

Her head dropped and, unable to look me in the eye, she said, "I am so ashamed, Anne, but I need to tell you that I suffer from bulimia." Her shame was evidently painful for her. "I'm so sorry I haven't been able to admit it to you, until now." I could see she was hating herself for it and blaming herself as she couldn't control it, but, in fact, this was her regaining her own control, by being able say it out loud. This was the breakthrough that she needed so that she could slowly start to heal.

I told her how grateful I was that she had shared this with me and thanked her for telling me. Her relief was evident. She confessed that she had been concerned I would be disgusted with her. Slowly, I was able to console her and assured her that her telling someone marked the beginning of her recovery and that was the most important thing to me. She added that she had told a close friend who was helping her seek the right advice. I was happy to hear that. Moving from the feeling of being utterly alone to having support was another important step. And now there were two of us who knew and who would be there to help her. The relief on her face spoke for itself.

Diana explained that her bulimia had started when she had started attending important functions, particularly dinners where she had to sit down to eat. She was so nervous that she found it very hard to keep the food down and, after the evening was over and she was back home, she would start throwing up. A lot. Meeting so many people was terrifying to her and the feeling that she was being judged with every move she made or how she looked or what she said caused her to feel totally inadequate. Although she had gained more confidence over the years, there were still times where she resorted to the cycle of bulimia, because for a short time emptying herself made her feel better.

Understanding the disease was the way forward, I told her, adding that finding ways not to judge herself would come in time.

Over the years, there were numerous newspaper articles that had commented on how thin Diana looked at specific periods of her life and hinted at the idea that she had some kind of eating disorder. I had been concerned a few times when we met for class and she looked overly thin or had dark circles under her eyes. But any time I gently approached her with my concern, she would say she was just tired and thanked me for asking.

I recalled telling her the story of the dancer at the London City Ballet who had suffered from bulimia. Now, as I remembered, it was Diana who had raised the topic and expressed some concern about the young dancer. Naturally, I thought for a minute that maybe I should have been more forceful when suspecting there might be a problem. The truth was that she would have needed to be ready to hear my concern, and be open to needing help, essential steps in taking back control.

In any case, it was not helpful, dwelling on my guilt. We were now in the moment of recognizing what she was going through and my giving her support was the most important thing I could do. Diana had opened a floodgate of deep emotions, but I knew her discussing her bulimia would bring her clarity and give her different strength in time. I also knew that if this information were to become common knowledge, it would do her irreparable damage.

I gathered that the Palace had concerns and were aware, or at least suspected the problem. I realized that they may have been worried that it could be dangerous if anyone from the outside world found out. I concluded they were trying to keep things contained and to make sure the press never had confirmation of their suspicions, either about the marriage or the bulimia.

The more I thought, the angrier I felt. If the "establishment" knew definitively, had anyone reached out to offer help and guidance? It didn't seem that they had. Had they dismissed this disease as a sign of weakness, not understanding the mental anguish Diana was in? While Diana had not mentioned how she was being treated at the palace, she had told me that Charles was not supportive or understanding, even though she had tried to explain the reasons for it, including expressing the hurt she felt because he was spending so much time with Camilla Parker Bowles. She knew that her reactions to the situation aggravated her illness, which in turn contributed to their marital problems.

For me, the most important thing was that Diana, herself, was taking big steps towards her own healing.

CHAPTER TWENTY-FOUR

Who's for Tennis?

"DO YOU PLAY TENNIS?" was the question Diana asked me one day in early June at the beginning of the class. "Would you like to join me to play with Steffi Graf?"

I was dumbfounded.

My mother was an avid Wimbledon fan. During an important match on television, no one was allowed to talk. She would curse at the players if they missed a crucial shot. My siblings and I used to laugh at her demands that we be quiet and pay attention; and yet, because of that, I became a huge fan. Back then, I'd taken tennis lessons at the local club and loved it. But in recent years, I hadn't kept up.

It didn't take me very long to consider the offer. I knew I was not at that level and would be mortified with embarrassment if I were to play with Steffi Graf. I graciously declined, but told Diana I was very touched that she would ask me.

Steffi was in London for the Wimbledon Championships, which would get underway in a few weeks. She wanted to get acclimatized ahead of the tournament. She was only nineteen and had already won the Australian

Open earlier that year. She enjoyed playing on hard courts, clay courts, and grass courts, and had won championships on all of them, which is a feat, as usually a player shined on only one or two types. Steffi won all four Grand Slams in 1988, as well as an Olympic gold medal.

Ironically, all these years later, it is my son who fell in love with tennis. He is now a tennis coach and has his own indoor tennis club in Toronto, which provides year-round tennis, and an outdoor club in Sierra Vista, Arizona. They are both called the Supreme Court Tennis Club, which gives you an idea of his sense of humour. His vision is to provide affordable tennis at the highest level and without making the sport elitist. One of the rules of his club is "no all-white clothing . . . we ain't that type of club."

I knew the strength of Alastair's commitment to the sport by the time he was sixteen, when he would discuss with me, at length, the quality of different tennis racquets. It reminded me of the same conversations I'd had with my mother, only about ballet shoes. His business savvy started at the same time. With a friend, he had invested in a stringing machine for tennis racquets and they ran a stringing business out of the garage. It was quite lucrative, even though they charged a nominal fee, completely undercutting the professional tennis shops that offered the service. They both learned a lot and loved perfecting the tension on a racquet for a specific player at the local club.

The Princess had thought and hoped that her time with Steffi was going to be a casual *hit*, as they say in the tennis world, but it turned into a media event for the opening of the prestigious Vanderbilt Racquet Club in downtown London. That same day, Wayne had invited Diana and me for lunch at his new home after the match.

Wayne's house was tucked away in the South Kensington neighbour-hood of London. It was a style known as a mews home. "Mews" is a term originating from royal stables that once existed near Charing Cross in London. Mews were originally intended to stable horses and carriages and would have living quarters above. The coach driver and ostlers, or coachmen, lived in the coach house on the same level as the stables. This was before the invention of the motorcar, so no traffic went through the mews street, and the streets were usually cobbled.

Wayne's house, located behind Queen's Gate, as it is known, was converted in the 1900s, like so many of these old houses. The mews is usually situated in the rear of what would have been an extravagant eighteenth- or nineteenth-century mansion. His living quarters are on one side, and you crossed a courtyard to enter the studio. You then made your way down a very grand staircase to arrive in the dance space, which was originally the ballroom of the main house.

I was thrilled when Wayne bought the property. I had known that it was for sale and had mentioned it to him because I knew he was looking for a space where he could live and still have a dance studio. Over time, Wayne did much to improve the building to make it habitable. He also redid the studio. I knew Diana would love the idea of being in this unique place.

The studio had been the old Andrew Hardie School of Dance, where I had spent time taking many classes. Andrew Hardie was a remarkable teacher with an incredible pedigree. He had worked with the Royal Academy of Dance. He also created a unique program to train athletes and strengthen their bodies, which included ballet exercises. When I worked with him, he was getting on in years but was still precise in his training. He would observe you, sitting with ballet master stick in hand, which he would use to emphasize a part of your body that maybe you were not using correctly. After the class, he would then spend time explaining how specific corrections in posture or movement would improve your dance.

I had arrived early to be there before the Princess, and to have a bit of time with Wayne. He had come back on a day off from his tour of *Song*

& Dance so he could host this special lunch. I presumed he was either bringing in a chef or was having food delivered. Silly me. When I got there, he told me he was cooking. He saw my reaction and laughed and said, "So you think I can't cook?" It had never occurred to me that he could. I had enjoyed many dinners with Wayne and George, but they were usually at some super restaurant that darling George had organized. George was Wayne's manager, who had also been invited for lunch. "I am making fish," said Wayne, speaking to us from the kitchen as some very pleasant smells were wafting our way. George and I exchanged warm giggles and shook our heads.

The table had been beautifully set for three in Wayne's dining room. Once the Princess and her detective, Ken Wharfe, arrived, George was going to take the officer across to the dance studio where they would have lunch. This would allow Diana to chat freely with us in Wayne's cozy, relaxed home. George was always caring and thoughtful.

Fortunately, the entrance to the mews was private. She was not in an official car, but driving her own car, accompanied by her detective. She "was incognito," she said, laughing, as George and I met her in the courtyard. After a quick greeting, she sprinted up the metal steps to say hello to Wayne, who popped his head out of the kitchen for a moment, shouting, "Sit down, I'll be right there!" Wayne was wonderfully casual. I could tell how much Diana enjoyed being treated like any member of the family popping round for a visit.

She had come straight from the match with Steffi and her face still had the warm glow of exercise. She was very glad to sit and relax, telling me that as she had managed to return a couple of shots. She added that maybe Steffi was being kind and let her off the hook a bit. Nonetheless, she had thoroughly enjoyed it and worked up a good sweat and appetite.

"I hope you're hungry," Wayne shouted from the kitchen.

"I'm starving," Diana shouted back.

A few minutes later, Wayne entered, wearing oven gloves and holding a dish with a trout lying on silver foil. He plonked the dish down on the table, rushing back to the kitchen for the vegetables. It was delightful. Once he sat down and we began our meal, I was able to enjoy the interactions between Wayne and Diana, appreciating how they always made each other laugh. It was infectious. Diana was happy not standing on ceremony, but really getting the chance to relax and talk. The conversation moved from tennis to dance, and to the pressures of performance that both brought into play. There was a great deal of banter and fun teasing of each other. Wayne had mastered an impersonation of John McEnroe for his show *Dash*. This led to a fun discussion about the process of having to study the subject before characterizing him in order to make it funny. An audience must immediately be able to recognize who it is, although in this case, the shorts and headband that are famous parts of McEnroe's tennis outfit did it immediately.

A gorgeous gâteau was presented for dessert, which Wayne admitted to having picked up at the local deli. That didn't matter. It was delicious and Diana wolfed down a generous slice.

George and Ken came across from the dance studio when it was time for Diana to go, but she wanted to stay a bit longer, so they sat down, too. Ken was telling jokes and making us all laugh. We showed Diana the dance studio, which she loved, of course, and we all enjoyed looking at the photographs on the wall.

By now it was nearly four. After offering to wash up and thanking Wayne for such a lovely lunch, she and Ken left so she could get back to Kensington Palace to be with her boys. It had been a wonderful, memorable afternoon for all of us.

CHAPTER TWENTY-FIVE

All I Ask of You!

A FEW WEEKS LATER, we had just finished our class and were lying on the floor to cool down and relax the muscles, when Diana sat up, announcing, "I have an idea I want to ask you about." Intrigued, I listened.

She started by saying how the experience of dancing on the Covent Garden stage had been fulfilling for her, but she had never really seen herself dance. "What would you say if we were to film me dancing, just for me to see, and maybe show to the boys? That way I would see my mistakes and it would be so wonderful to have."

Remember, this was in the days before iPhones, which today allow you to record a video of anything and see it back instantly. Recording was more complex in 1988, well before the days of smartphones. I knew her idea would require some thought. I didn't own a suitable camera and would probably need a trustworthy colleague who was an experienced cameraman, as I would want to watch so as to get the best angles. Probably lighting would be needed, and what would I do for the post-production and editing of the film? I wouldn't want the material to be in anyone else's hands but mine.

I presumed that we would do the filming in the dance studio, but then realized that would mean other people would know where we did our classes and, since it was an ideal location, I did not want to risk that. Diana was continuing to chat as I was thinking through things, my mind swirling when she asked, "Could we do it on the *Phantom* stage?" I certainly wasn't expecting that. Laughing, she said, "Do you think it's possible?" I knew the experience of being on stage again would be thrilling for her, but this was going to be quite complex to pull off.

We agreed that the first steps were to start to prepare what material we would use and how much rehearsal we would need to perfect a routine. I told her that I would treat her like any dancer preparing for a performance, which delighted her. She left that day beaming and with the understanding that I would see if I could come up with a plan and tell her at the next class.

Now I was in the biggest dilemma. How on earth was I going to make this happen and keep it quiet? A mild panic hit me at the possible circumstances that could arise.

I knew I had access to the stage at Her Majesty's Theatre, where *Phantom* was playing, because I took understudy rehearsals every week, usually on Thursdays and Fridays. I would need permission to use the stage if it wasn't for a rehearsal. What would I say? "Oh, I'm bringing Diana, the Princess of Wales, to do a wee dance!" I laughed to myself at how absurd that might seem. "Oh, and by the way, I'm bringing a film crew and will need lighting, which means I will also need a tech crew, and, regarding music, can I use the sound system, which means I will need a sound technician, and can I have a dressing room for the Princess? And, yes, there will be some detectives on hand. By the way, don't tell the press because we want to keep it private!" It was such a ridiculous notion. But, somehow, I wanted to pull it off.

My mind was in a whirl over the next few days as I tried to work out all the possible challenges and the best approach. I knew I could put a small camera crew together with the help of my husband and our contacts. We did not need to tell the team what or who we were filming until they saw for themselves on the day. Three cameras would be ideal to cover all potential shots, but I decided on just one cameraman who could move around. The fewer people, the better. We would repeat the dance so the cameraman could shoot it from different angles. The Princess would need to build her stamina and we would have to ensure the dance combination was not overly long. We could also shoot the dance in segments. We could book the team and give needed information nearer to the time.

I still had to solve the theatre question. I did not want to ask the theatre management just yet. I needed a backup plan for an alternative space to film in case management did not agree.

I explained the plan to Diana at the next class, suggesting that perhaps we could use Wayne's studio if there was a problem—not that I had checked with Wayne, but I knew him well enough to know that he would agree. Diana thought it was brilliant. We laughed a lot at all the scheming we had to do. Diana said she would let her lady-in-waiting know the details closer to the date. I was glad of that, because I did need someone official to know about it. I certainly didn't want all the responsibility. I did, however, worry that Anne might not approve and would try to stop it. We had never had a follow-up conversation after her phone call to me about ending the dance classes.

I didn't want to make the filming date too far away, but also needed several weeks to choreograph, teach, and rehearse the dance. It was important to make sure we were building momentum with each class leading up to the big day. In August, I was due to fly to Madrid, followed by Greece for a show Wayne was doing, so I wanted to complete this mad project before then. We were just at the end of June, so there was enough time. I hoped.

Diana and I settled on the choice of music and choreography, and she worked hard on endurance, style, and performance. I would give her feedback, or notes, as we call them, to adjust or improve the movement, and she would repeat the combination again and again to perfect it, loving every minute of it. I continued to treat her like a professional working towards a debut, which she greatly appreciated.

I approached Howard Harrison about using the stage and theatre auditorium for the filming, as it would mean cancelling understudy rehearsals on the day of the shoot. Howard was part of the management team of the Really Useful Group, Andrew Lloyd Webber's business. He was always helpful when I asked him about any matter regarding *Phantom*. He was completely on board, but wanted to share it with Nick Allot, who was in a higher position of authority and was close to Cameron Mackintosh and Andrew. I stressed the importance of it being kept confidential and he said, "Mum's the word!" Nick was receptive as well and, because of their support, we got permission to use the theatre and anything else we needed. They remained discreet throughout. I explained that I needed a closed set, which meant no one coming on stage for the two hours I had scheduled for the shoot. They obliged.

The day of filming arrived. I was there early to supervise "the get in." The cameraman still did not know what or who we were filming; he set up comfortably, taking in all the potential areas where he could achieve the best shots. The only information I had given him was that it was a dance excerpt, which does require the expertise of a cameraman who understands movement.

The stage had been left open, with all set pieces pushed away and a bright lighting cue on. I had decided just to go with our usual sound system, my tape recorder and a couple of speakers, so as to not bring any more attention than necessary to what we were doing. Also, I did not want the music to play over the sound system, known as the Tannoy, to the dressing rooms. The Tannoy is extremely useful during performance. It allows the actors in their dressing rooms to hear what is happening on stage, so, if they have a long break between scenes, they can gauge how much time they have to be ready for their next entrance. I thought that it was unlikely that actors would be in the dressing rooms, since it was the day after a two-show day and the actors would most likely be resting for the evening performance. Still, I wanted to make sure that no one heard the music we were using.

There was a quick-change dressing room that Diana would use in the backstage area on the stage level, with a washroom nearby.

All was set. Diana arrived at the stage door with Anne Beckwith-Smith and, of course, the detectives. She was quickly brought to the stage area, where I met her. She had visited the backstage on a few occasions, so the doorman was not particularly suspicious of her entering. He smiled warmly when he saw her.

Diana's face was glowing as she stood at centre stage, taking in the ambience, and looking out at the grandeur of the chandelier. I walked her down to the stalls so she could see the stage through the lens of the camerman's equipment. The surprise on his face was delightful when I introduced him to Diana. I deliberately left him alone for a minute to gather himself, if needed, when Diana returned to the stage. He remained completely professional and treated it like it was any other gig.

We started the filming with a rehearsal. This allowed the cameraman to see how the dance moved and how he would be able to capture the best angles and light. After a few adjustments, we were ready for the first take. I knew that we would probably not use it because some nerves were showing, but that was my way of getting them out of the way. It is a very different feel when dancing on a stage in a solo dance without the feedback of an audience. There is no applause when you finish and you are left to judge whether what you had just danced was good or not. That's why it is better to have a trusted, knowledgeable eye, who can correct, comment, and encourage. The second take was better, and Diana started to relax and have some fun.

Anne Beckwith-Smith stayed close to me and was wonderful about running to the front of the stage in case Diana needed anything in between takes, which allowed me time to talk to the cameraman. Anne had a great smile on her face and was very supportive. She could see how much Diana enjoyed dancing.

I had organized water, which Diana was glad of, but told her just to take sips between takes, keeping hydrated but not bloating herself. She touched up her make-up with a quick look in the mirror and a dab of powder.

I'd known the time would go very quickly and it did. I felt we hadn't quite nailed everything, so I was rather a taskmaster, but the fact is that once it's on film you can't correct it. I knew I had to be strict to get the best performance. We did multiple takes, and I was feeling much happier with what I was seeing.

Anne came to me to say that Her Royal Highness was getting very tired, and I realized that, but pushed for one final take, in which Diana rose to the occasion, giving it her all. It had been a more intense session than Diana realized, but she had learned what it takes to make it to performance level on film.

After a quick change of her clothes, we slipped her out the stage door and she got into the waiting car, sweaty and hot, but with such a look of satisfaction on her flushed face.

A bit later, I managed to quietly leave the theatre with all the film handed over by the cameraman, whose broad smile told me that it had been a pleasure. How lucky I was to have such a great man who totally understood the need for privacy? He said that keeping it private was not going to be a problem since probably no one would believe him anyway.

By evening, it had hit the press. Various newspaper headlines shouted out that Diana had danced to "All I Ask of You" on the *Phantom* stage! The articles went on to say that Andrew Lloyd Webber was there, Sarah Brightman sang, and Gillian Lynne had choreographed the number and was overseeing the filming. The most alarming piece of sensationalism the press had managed to conjure was that it was to be an anniversary gift for Diana's husband, Charles. The fairy tale was still alive, seven years later!

"All I Ask of You" is a beautiful, heartfelt love song that was created by Andrew Lloyd Webber for his wife, Sarah Brightman, who played Christine Daaé in *The Phantom of the Opera*, with lyrics by Charles Hart and Richard Stilgoe, and it is gloriously romantic. But, no, it is not what Diana danced to. Nor did she sing!

The music that we used was the anthem from the 1986 movie *Top Gun*. Its instrumental rock music with solo electric guitar played by Steve Stevens is very uplifting. We had used it in class; Diana found it very inspiring, and I wanted something she was familiar with.

I was flabbergasted at the press coverage and how much had been completely made up. It was mind-blowing. It did show me how far the press would go—even to complete fabrication—to get a story on Diana and to ultimately sell a newspaper. Diana had just wanted to be able to see herself dance, and it certainly was not an anniversary gift.

I giggled to myself when I saw the newspapers on my way home, and laughed even more when I realized the false headlines meant that we had pulled it off. The press obviously didn't have the right story, they just knew something had taken place.

Arriving home, my husband and I shared a celebratory drink. Then I had the job of editing the material. Over the next few days, he and I sat together and worked. I was so glad of his help. There was a lot of material to go through. We didn't use a slate to number the takes, but just ran the film. We chose the best take, which became the master, then added different angles to keep the viewing sharp. Overall, I was pleased, but knew there were still some adjustments I would have liked to have made with more time. But isn't it always like that? The last step was finishing the credits. I had the greatest fun naming Palace Productions as the producers.

I handed the final cut on a VHS tape to the Princess at the next class (which makes me laugh as I write this, because VHS is now all but extinct). We both reminisced about what a terrific afternoon it had been, and Diana told me she was truly exhausted after filming, collapsed in a hot bath, and hadn't moved for the next few hours. She couldn't wait to to see the results on screen. Naturally, I was terrified that she might not like it.

I then had to fly off to Europe to do Wayne's show. I received this letter on my return:

I couldn't be <u>more</u> thrilled with the video and how I laugh every time I see the credits!

I see a lot of mistakes as do William & Harry who have great enjoyment pointing out mummy with her head down or "why aren't you smiling."

I hated cancelling our lesson for Tuesday but with the boys here it was difficult to up and go—

CHAPTER TWENTY-SIX

Afterwards

I WAS THRILLED THAT Diana was pleased with the video. That meant the world to me, as did the ongoing secret of our precious meetings in the dance studio, which continued with very few people knowing about them.

I then got a call from Buckingham Palace asking me to meet Anne Beckwith-Smith at the offices. In all the years I had been with the Princess, I never had been asked there, so it felt a bit strange and a little suspicious. My gut told me to be on my guard.

On arriving, I was shown into Anne's office. She warmly welcomed me and thanked me for arranging the filming for Her Royal Highness and said, of course, that they would take care of the expenses involved. The Princess had wanted to make sure I wasn't out of pocket. For that I was very grateful. I didn't expect payment for the dance classes, as my sister who was in the diplomatic service had told me that it wasn't quite done. I had been paid for the first few classes in 1981 because they had asked me to send an invoice, but I had never submitted invoices after that. It didn't seem appropriate. My relationship with Diana had come to mean more. The Princess would give me lovely personal gifts–Butler & Wilson earrings, a special doll for Emily, baby gifts, and beautifully ornate Asprey eggs.

For some reason I knew there was something beyond a thank-you coming in this meeting, and it did.

Anne asked me to make sure that I submitted every piece of film that was taken on the day of filming. It turns out that *they* wanted to make sure the film did not get into the wrong hands. I was irate. My loyalty was being questioned, and being a Scot, loyalty and trust are huge things. I had been with the Princess for more than seven years, and it was still not common knowledge that I was her dancing teacher or that she took dancing classes. Why was this being questioned in this way? I had to speak my mind. I asked Anne why this was being requested. She was very apologetic and explained that she had been asked by the Palace to ensure discretion. I realized that probably her hands were tied; the request was coming from higher up. Maybe *they* were terrified that the press might get hold of the footage. I could see the potential problems that would cause.

I was still seething at the implication that I might give material to a TV channel or newspaper. When I bade Anne goodbye, I did not hide how offensive the request was to me. It left a sour taste in my mouth.

It was many years later that this incident came to light again. I was working on a show just outside of Toronto and staying at a hotel the theatre company had put me up in. It was after the 1992 release of the Andrew Morton book, *Diana: Her True Story.* I was sitting in my room prepping for the day when the phone rang and the voice at the other end said, "Hello, Anne, this is Andrew Morton."

My immediate response was "Hello Andrew, it's taken you quite a while to find me." But I was thinking to myself, *How on earth did he discover where I was?* He had somehow reached my agent and my agent, thinking it was important, had given him the hotel number. There had never been any contact before.

His book had caused a sensation when it was released, stirring up a lot of controversy for its revelations of the breakdown of the royal marriage. The information had come from Diana herself, but I also knew from reading that a lot of his information was purely speculative. Certainly, the information on Diana's dance classes was not accurate. There seemed to be some guess work. After some polite chat, mainly from him, he said, "I understand there is a video of Diana dancing that you might have."

I was stunned and said nothing.

He went on. "That kind of material would be so valuable for people to know about and see."

I did not reply.

"Do you have the video?" he asked.

Still no reply from me. He asked the question again.

A very long pause ensued. I finally said, "Well, Andrew, maybe I do and maybe I don't."

He pressed on the importance of something like that being of great value to the public. I repeated my statement, "Maybe I do and maybe I don't."

Finally, he knew he was getting nowhere and concluded the call. "I'll give you a number that you can reach me at, Anne, if you would like to contact me at any time."

I put the phone down and took a deep breath. I would never call him.

It was hard to believe that so many years had passed since the filming of the video. The Andrew Morton book had done much to make the royal divorce inevitable. Andrew was obviously searching for additional material for his new edition, which was released after Diana's death.

For me, the constant sensationalism of the press, journalists, and writers made me angry. At that time, there was no way that I was saying or revealing anything about what had been a very special time with Diana.

CHAPTER TWENTY-SEVEN

A Constant Escalation

S HORTLY AFTER THE completion of the video in August, the Princess went on vacation with her family to Spain as guests of King Juan Carlos and Queen Sofia. The press footage did much to keep up the narrative that Charles and Diana's family life was intact. It showed Diana holding her sons' hands as they stood on either side of her. She looked happy and relaxed, as she always was when with her boys. Nothing gave her more joy.

Nevertheless, Diana had told me before leaving that having time together as a family had become extremely difficult, mainly due to schedules, but she also felt that her husband was deliberately avoiding having private time with her as a couple. This greatly upset her. She still loved her husband and wanted more than anything to rekindle the spark between them and put their troubles behind them. She wished to keep her family together, and was willing to work at it. Before she left on vacation, she believed it could happen.

When we discussed the vacation, she expressed her hopes that, after the photos had been taken, she and Charles would have a chance to be away from the glare of the public and away from both of their constant work demands. Diana anticipated that relaxing in the hot summer climate of the Mediterranean, surrounded by sea and beauty, would clear the air and help them find a positive way forward.

I knew there had been many times before when Diana had tried to bring romance back into their lives. On one occasion, I listened heartbroken to a story that she shared with me about an incident that had happened the previous year.

To revive and reunite as husband-and-wife, Diana had thought that a lovely lunch with just the two of them, relaxing together in privacy, would be appreciated by Charles. She planned an outdoor picnic at their country home at Highgrove House in the idyllic Gloucestershire countryside. She knew how much Charles loved being there. He spent hours planning and designing its organic farm and gardens, and was beginning to see the results of his work. Diana loved that gardening brought out his passion, as dance did for her.

On this occasion there was to be no one else around and no staff on hand. The table had been set outside and Diana was excitedly waiting for him. When Charles arrived, she eagerly expressed how happy she was to have some quiet time with him and, taking his hand, led him to the picnic she had arranged outside. Seeing the table set, he immediately dropped her hand and said, "*I don't eat outside.* Get the butler to take it all in immediately!" In that instant, she told me, a bit more of her died. Her loving intention was destroyed by a few strong words.

Whether or not he liked to eat outside, I could see that his lack of sensitivity stabbed her in some vulnerable place. During our classes in the weeks that followed the vacation, it was becoming much clearer to Diana that they were leading separate lives, and that this was what Charles wanted. She said she was at a loss of what to do. I could see it eating away at her, exacerbating the bulimia, deeply affecting her well-being, both emotionally and physically, as she tried to figure out the best course of action. What was especially difficult, she said, was knowing that Charles was spending his free time with Camilla, who seemed to provide him with whatever he felt was missing in his marriage.

As for me, I was angry and had many questions running through my head. Did Charles think that this was acceptable behaviour, and that Diana should just turn her back and ignore what was going on? Was he relieved that his wife was in her own extramarital affair? Did it affect him at all? It didn't seem so.

To be clear, Charles and Camilla's relationship had been reignited years before. It was long into the marriage before Diana even contemplated finding another way of having love and companionship in her life. She expressed to me that the affair caused her to have incredible guilt, and, yes, she knew she was aggravating the situation. Her intention had been to win her husband back by trying to make him jealous. It completely backfired. Charles seemed content with the situation, as it took the onus off him.

They say there are two sides to every story and I was only privy to Diana's. Outside of my own private questions, it was not for me to comment on what Charles was thinking or going through, but I was keenly aware of the deep hurt, anxiety, irreparable harm, and destruction he was causing Diana. She had convinced herself that she was the failure. She kept asking herself what she had done wrong to cause him not to love her. Her confidence was completely shattered. She found herself crying, more and more.

Over the next few months, we would have more serious discussions while sitting on the studio floor after class. Diana's marriage was always the central subject matter. I could see how intensely difficult it was for her as she grappled with what to do. It would be several more months before she found the courage to take the action that would change how she saw herself.

CHAPTER TWENTY-EIGHT

City of Music

IN NOVEMBER 1988, my working career took me to Vienna, which meant that Diana and I had to say goodbye for a few weeks. My heart was heavy for her, but, as always, with dignity, she assured me she would be fine and said she was thankful to be able to share her problems with me.

It was going to be hard for me to be away from my children, but the necessity of earning a living drove that decision, and I was extremely lucky to be doing work that I loved. My sister-in-law was staying in the house along with my husband to look after the two little ones while I was away, so I knew they were in good caring hands. My daughter, Emily, now eleven, was coming for a visit for a few days towards the end of my stay in Vienna to allow her a deserved special treat. She would be flying by herself for the first time and felt very grown up about that.

I was mounting the choreography and staging to produce *Das Phantom der Oper*. It was the first foreign production, set to open at the Theater an der Wien, and it was going to be a challenge for me as I only spoke *ein bisschen*—a little bit—of the language, which I had picked up on my first job out of ballet school at a German ballet company. It had been a bit of a harrowing experience as I tried to navigate my new life in Germany at age nineteen, but I had embraced it while trying to learn the language. The little knowledge I had of the German language would certainly help now.

I adored being in Vienna, the City of Music, as it's known, home of the greatest composers of the world, significantly Ludwig van Beethoven. He had lived for two years in a rent-free apartment inside the famous theatre where *Phantom* was to play. It was where he had composed some of his most magnificent pieces. He had spent a great deal of his life in Vienna. Imagining him walking along the old cobblestone streets with music running through his mind filled me with inspiration and made rehearsals an absolute joy.

The city also boasted the magnificent architecture of the Imperial Palace, the provocative art of Gustav Klimt, and, as I looked out on to the Danube River, I couldn't help but think of the beautiful waltzes of Johann Strauss. His joyful "Blue Danube" was something I often heard in ballet classes. To be in the world where his music was composed was awe-inspiring.

I arrived in Vienna several weeks before Gillian Lynne so I could set up her choreography and staging work with the new cast. The teaching and perfecting would take time for us all to rehearse, and it would be necessary to build up the cast's performance to the point that it was ready for Gillian's arrival. The anticipation and expectation of the choreographer's approval would do much to lift the standard of the performance; the performers knew Gillian's pedigree and that she would demand the best of them. Fortunately, after watching a first rehearsal with a very keen eye, Gillian was pleased with what she saw. She was then ready to dive into the masterclass rehearsal, adding her artistry and adjusting the dancers' movements to what best served a specific actor or as she saw fit. Her gregarious personality gave the cast an extra boost.

Gillian and I had always enjoyed our time together both in rehearsal and privately over many dinners. One very cold day, before opening and prior to my daughter's arrival, and when we were in preview performances, Gillian wanted to do some Christmas shopping. We walked through Stephansplatz where St. Stephen's Cathedral, one of the tallest cathedrals in the world, boldly dominated the skyline. The Christmas atmosphere was everywhere. We had a wonderful time choosing family gifts and then Gillian insisted on taking me to an early dinner. We chose a cozy-looking bar. She ordered two brandies "to warm us up." I had never experienced an alcoholic drink in the afternoon. This one was very memorable, not only for the inner warmth from the brandy but listening to Gillian's plan to see the famous Beethoven Steps, which were somewhere in the theatre and not open to the public. She had been hatching this plan for a while and wanted to make it happen before the opening night.

A few days later, thanks to her wonderful persistence and coercion, her wish was granted. The steps were almost hidden in a backstage area, carefully guarded under lock and key to preserve them. We had to walk through a dressing room to reach them. The anticipation we both felt was exhilarating. The man escorting us turned the key and opened a door to reveal a very dark stairwell with a small curve to the staircase as it spiraled upward. You could imagine Beethoven's very footsteps on the deep indents on each step. These stairs led him to his apartment and to his piano, where he created some of his most celebrated symphonies. His only opera, *Fidelio*, had its premiere in 1805 in the theatre below him. I will always be grateful to Gillian for that thrill.

Emily arrived a few days before opening night, which she was going to attend as my guest. She had loved flying. The attendant had been kind to her and didn't treat her like a child. At eleven, she was completely enamoured with living in the hotel, but she was at her happiest walking with me as we explored the magical Christmas markets together.

I realize now how much her early experiences of watching the ballet dancers at the London City Ballet or in *Phantom* or just being in a theatre influenced her work. She is now an artist and reflects on those experiences while describing her own art: "I loved the lines in the dancers' bodies. The gentle but powerful movements. I wanted to capture each pose."

Opening night of *Phantom* was a glittering evening, and a huge success. The musical would be performed in this theatre for another five years. Since then, it has returned many times for limited runs.

Despite the wonderful time I was having with Emily, I was looking forward to returning home. Naturally, I was very worried about Diana's situation and how things had gone while I was away. Her official visit to Paris with Charles in November, which occurred while I was in Vienna, had shown a radiant woman who appeared relaxed. Even though my greatest wish was that they would reconcile, I knew in my heart that this was probably not going to be the case. They were both abidingly good at disguising the discord between them on official visits. Charles was always shown as walking ahead of Diana as protocol demanded. She laughed once, telling me, "I see a lot of the back of my husband's head!" I was also anxious to return to the sanctuary of class with Diana, which would be after Christmas.

Upon arriving home, after the most wonderful hugs and kisses from my wee darlings who had arranged a welcome home tea party for Mummy and Emily, with every stuffed animal they could find in attendance, my sister-in-law asked if she could have a few private words with me. I immediately worried that there had been problems with the children because I was away, but that was not the case. The children had been wonderful, and she had loved being with them. Her concern was that my husband was under emotional stress. She felt that he was masking some personal issues and further suspected that there were financial difficulties. She was worried and concerned that it might affect the children and me, so she had wanted to alert me in a way of protecting us all.

I was reeling and felt faint. I had to sit down. I knew from her intensity that there was something serious going on. She said, considerately and compassionately, "Please talk to my brother." When I did, very late that evening after he got home, it revealed the reality of my troubling situation. Ultimately, it would lead me to making some very difficult decisions.

My Christmas would be quiet. I was happy just to be with the children and at home.

While I was away, my husband and I had received an invitation to the Kensington Palace Christmas party, but since it was on December 13, I could not attend. The royal Christmas card had also arrived in the post, along with a a special gift from Diana, the most beautiful Halcyon Days enamel trinket box. On the front it read "Christmas 1988," and inside a personal inscription read "Lots of love at Christmas from Diana." A card with a beautiful note was also enclosed—"To someone very special who I couldn't do without!"—which did much to keep my spirits up.

CHAPTER TWENTY-NINE

Confidence and Confrontation

THE TRADITIONS OF bringing in the New Year in Scotland are well known—putting the past behind us and stepping into the New Year with new beginnings, making a fresh start—and that was exactly what I resolved to do as 1989 began.

I was excited to get back into dance class with Diana, who had spent Christmas at Sandringham with her family. It made me smile to see the TV newscast showing William and Harry exploring an old fire engine after the royal family custom of attending church together. On that first class in January 1989, we wished each other a happy New Year and enjoyed talking about the importance of New Year's resolutions and moving forward. She told me that she had had a marvellous time with her children over the holiday and, in her words, that "she and Charles were civil to each other."

I thought it important that we should have an enjoyable dance class, so I had chosen a Scottish lament for our lyrical jazz adagio after the warm-up. Diana loved dancing to the romance in the music in her favourite style of dance; it was less constricting and more open to interpretation. The class evolved into a Scottish theme as Diana wanted to know more about the Scottish country dances and Highland dances, what they were called and the origins of the different steps. We were both in a state of giggles as she tried a Highland fling. I taught her the correct positioning and meaning behind the arms, where the shape of the arm and specific holding of the fingers represented a stag's antlers. She loved hearing about the sword dance, which requires precision and agility. Highland warriors performed the sword dance before going into battle and, if their feet touched a sword, it was a bad omen. "It makes so much more sense to me now," she said gratefully.

The Princess was due to go on a three-day solo visit to New York City at the beginning of February. She was looking forward to it, even though it was going to be a whirlwind. As patron of the Welsh National Opera, she had agreed to attend the American debut performance of *Falstaff* at BAM, as it's known in the theatre world—the Brooklyn Academy of Music. The white satin gown that she wore for the evening highlighted her elegance and dazzled the audience. I knew that Diana was not an opera lover, much preferring to watch ballet or other dance performances. She told me on her return that although the performance of *Falstaff* ran long, thankfully "it's a comedy, which certainly helped!"

She loved her time in New York "as people were so welcoming, very kind and open, not at all stuffy," was how she put it. "It made me feel relaxed and confident."

As she talked, it became clear that the trip had affected her. She was struck more than anywhere else by the stark contrast between the rich Americans attending the gala after the performance and her heart-breaking visit to the Henry Street Settlement in the Lower East Side. "I saw Harlem for the first time," she said, "and driving there was an eye-opener. Meeting the children who have AIDS was distressing for me."

I could see from the news coverage that Diana exuded empathy and compassion as she spent time with the children at the settlement. That was not a hard thing for Diana. Her genuineness was evident. Her presence once again helped to recognize the seriousness of this disease.

What felt especially different for Diana about the trip was that she was not trailing behind her husband or anxious for his approval. Instead, she was out there in the world and felt worthy in her own right. It was symbolic for her and had opened her eyes to what could be possible in the future.

I was due to have my first visit to New York, which I was very excited about, so I was pleased to have the chance to speak to Diana about how she experienced it, even though it was quite different from what I would be doing or how I'd be travelling. I was going to see the Broadway production of *Phantom* because later that year I would mount the musical in Toronto. Gillian wanted me to take note of any moments in the performance that veered away from the original production. This would help her figure out what she would incorporate into the Canadian production.

I arrived in New York and pinched myself when I first saw Times Square. There I was, in the heart of Broadway, on my way to the Majestic Theatre on 44th Street. The energy was electric, it was so alive, bustling with theatregoers on their way to musicals and plays that evening. Passing the famous 42nd Street, which has a musical named for it, I beamed in delight. Little did I know that I would end up spending a lot of a time in New York, working on the production of different musicals.

On my return to London a week or so later, I could see Diana's confidence was growing. Since she had confronted her bulimia, she was slowly healing from its triggers and patterns. She had started to reclaim her life, finding the courage to finally make her stand. She told me that things had not changed in her marriage, and she found herself getting more and more riled and angered, instead of upset. Charles had become blatant about spending time with his own circle of friends, with Camilla often invited, and Diana not. It was becoming humiliating for her.

The exclusion seemed to be widely known in the close circle of royalty. Diana expressed to me that everybody believed she would simply accept that it was fine for Charles to have a mistress and do what a lot of other wives have done in the past: say nothing and create their own lives, remaining the dutiful spouse in public. Diana knew she had become brilliant at playing the role of dutiful wife, and she did not, in any way, want the monarchy harmed or to cause the slightest bit of hurt to her children. But she had decided to make a stand.

I vividly remember her telling me, as we sat in the downstairs studio, that it was time to face her fears and confront the problem, but not her husband. She was going to ask the woman he was spending most of his time with to leave her husband alone to give her marriage a chance. This was not a spur of the moment idea. It was a calculated move, and it included the element of surprise for the woman in question.

Diana knew that there was to be a birthday party for Camilla's sister, Annabel Elliot, which Diana was not expected to attend. She decided she would turn up. Charles was already there. When she walked into the room, there was an awkward look of surprise from the guests and some cumbersome conversation as everyone tried to remain polite; "everyone" being mostly members of the Charles and Camilla set.

As the evening went on, Diana noticed that neither Charles nor Camilla was anywhere to be seen in the upstairs rooms where the party was being held. Her instinct told her they were together downstairs. She decided she would go and see for herself. Her loyal detective, Ken Wharfe, was with her and tried to suggest otherwise, but she knew her moment was coming. She made her way down the stairs, her heart pounding in anticipation, but she was determined to achieve what she came to do.

Diana had always found Camilla quite frightening, a woman fourteen years her senior with a cocksure demeanour that intimidated her. But not tonight. Diana found them in the company of other guests in the downstairs living room. There was a jarring silence as Diana entered the room, followed by some polite exchanges. Diana asked everyone to leave, including Charles, as she would like a word with Camilla. To see them scurry was laughable, she told me. She sat down close to Camilla and looked her straight in the eyes and said that she wasn't born yesterday, and she knew what was going on. Camilla looked at her claiming innocence, which gave Diana the fuel to keep going. At one point Camilla made a very strange comment that further propelled Diana. "You have everything in the world," Camilla said. "Men falling for you and two beautiful children. What more could you want?"

"I want my husband," was Diana's firm reply.

"I did it, I did it, Anne!" she announced, as she related to me the events of that momentous night. I thoroughly enjoyed hearing every detail, but more than anything loved Diana's brave and bold accomplishment. She and Charles had driven home together, and "he was all over me like a little boy who has done something wrong and is wanting back in your good books."

The Camilla confrontation is now well documented, with Diana herself relating the story to Andrew Morton. She told me that she had cried many tears that night, but they were tears of relief and emotion that had been waiting to come out. "I feel a tremendous shift, Anne, in myself." I could not have been more delighted.

CHAPTER THIRTY

A Very Difficult Decision

HER ACTIONS HAD bolstered Diana's confidence. She had hopeful expectations that the confrontation might change things with her husband. Would Camilla do the decent and right thing and walk away to give Charles and Diana's marriage a chance?

In her heart, Diana doubted that would happen. If nothing changed, she would forge ahead to create an independent life for herself and her children, while still being the Princess of Wales. This conclusion was definitive for her at that time. The true Diana was shining through. She would embark on the future with new conviction.

In March, Diana and Charles made their official royal visit to the United Arab Emirates to promote British trade. The world saw a very self-assured Diana. Her now iconic fashion choices made a confident statement with every outfit. She was an unparalleled ambassador for Britain.

By April, it had become apparent that I was facing a very difficult decision of my own. The beginning of it was to face the harsh reality that I would have to sell my house in Sunninghill and move to something more affordable. After considering many options, the best choice I had was to move back to Glasgow, where house prices were much more reasonable. I would have to find work and take on more of it, in whatever form that took, so having the support of my family would be incredibly helpful, especially since they would be able to help with the little ones. My mother was an absolute rock, and I knew I could depend on her.

My husband had lost his job many months before, and it was now becoming clear to me that he was a high-functioning alcoholic. How naive could I have been not to have seen it? I wanted to get him some help and give things a chance to resolve themselves. I hoped a move could be the answer to a new beginning. It was a most conflicting time for me, but, after weeks of consideration, it seemed that this was the best choice I could make under the circumstances. I was extremely sad, as it meant I would have to leave the Princess. Thinking of the last beautiful note she had sent me at Christmas filled me with anguish, especially the thought that I might be letting her down. I knew, however, that I had to put the well-being of my family first.

I also knew that later in the year, in August 1989, I was committed to mount *Phantom* in Toronto. I had conducted auditions there the year before, in 1988, returning to the city for a few days at a time with the creative team to complete casting for a stellar Canadian cast, except for the three leads. Rebecca Caine who had been the alternate, performing two shows a week in the London production, was to play Christine. The dashing Byron Nease, who was an American, was to play Raoul, and the exceptional Irish tenor Colm Wilkinson was to play the title role.

Colm had been the first person to sing *Phantom* material for Andrew Lloyd Webber, at his home in Sydmonton in 1985, a year before the musical hit the stage. Gillian had attended that evening and had told me that it was an extraordinary experience hearing him. "He has a voice from God," she remembered.

From the moment I had stepped off the plane, to the warm air hitting me, I fell in love with Toronto again. My first visit had been in the early seventies, when I was there on a sabbatical from the Scottish Ballet to take classes with the National Ballet and Lois Smith. I had enjoyed the relaxed atmosphere and the Canadian way of life.

A decade later, the Toronto musical theatre scene was developing into something very exciting. The production of *Phantom* was to be at the magnificently restored Pantages Theatre. This undertaking was led by the brilliant producer Garth Drabinsky. The Pantages served as the epitome of splendour and style, housing *Phantom* for its run, which would last a full ten years.

Garth showed tremendous interest in every aspect of producing the show, joining me in early auditions to become acquainted with all that was required to maintain the highest level of excellence. He had shown me around the theatre as it was being restored and I could tell his love for art and architecture matched the love he had for performers. I remember asking about the rehearsal rooms and if he knew where they were. I was told that there wasn't enough space for them, but he promised to rectify that in the next theatre he would build, and he did.

It was going to be nearly a two-month rehearsal schedule, starting in August, and it offered a lucrative contract that helped my situation. Management was willing to rent a house for me and the family so I decided we would all move to the city for the duration of my contract and have the experience of a new country. I was also hopeful that it would be a healing time. With the contract confirmed, I was able to quickly sell the house in Sunninghill. I managed to buy an affordable place in Glasgow, and we planned to have everything moved in before the trip to Toronto.

I next had to find the right moment to inform the Princess. When I told her, explaining all the reasons I found myself making this very difficult decision, she was most understanding. Her concern was for my well-being. She was deeply respectful, knowing how complicated the choice had been for me to make. She did not pry, but wanted me to know that she was there to talk to if I needed. "God knows I've bent your ear off so many times," she said. "I shall miss you dreadfully." I asked her if she would like me to recommend a new dance teacher for her. She said, "No, it would not be the same." We agreed we would just enjoy our dancing classes over the next couple of months, which we thoroughly did.

On Sunday, June 25, 1989, a royal gala, in the gracious presence of HRH the Princess of Wales, was planned in celebration of Wayne's *World of Dance*. I would only have one more class with the Princess after that, so the evening would be a highlight for me, the crowning of our shared time together in the Princess's official capacity. The show would be the last time I would work with Wayne, assisting him, and leading rehearsals. The show was a collection of Wayne's favourite moments from his dance career and featured snippets from shows with many different styles of dance, and of course, a lot of humorous skits, which the audience always loved.

The evening was a benefit performance for the children's charity Variety, in aid of the Malcolm Sargent Cancer Fund, of which the Princess was patron. It was the perfect way to celebrate a special evening.

My family had been invited to attend. My mother was going to come from Scotland with my eldest sister, Georgina. One of my other sisters, Feona, who lived close to me, would attend with her husband. My family had always been exceptionally loyal and never told anyone that I gave dance classes to Diana. They could sense that sometimes I was worried for the Princess, but never pushed to know more. To be with my Scottish family at this performance meant a great deal to me.

As it was an official gala, all the ladies were required to wear long gowns. I decided to rent a dress for the evening as I didn't want any additional wardrobe to take to Scotland—I was downsizing for the move. I chose a strapless lemon gown that flared with an A-line at the hips. I made sure it was not so long that I tripped over it. We all met and left together from my house in Sunninghill in a black limousine and travelled to the Royalty Theatre in London.

We were on a high, loving every bit of the journey. When we arrived at the theatre, the atmosphere was electric. I had to slip backstage to quickly check that everyone was all right and wish the performers good luck. There was the usual nervous excitement, which was healthy, and would make for a great performance. Once I had said my hellos, I went to find my family, who were waiting outside the theatre, enjoying the entrances of various dignitaries. Since we all had to be seated before the Princess arrived, we then made our own way into the theatre.

My enjoyment of the evening came not so much from what was happening on stage as the bliss of sharing it with my family, people that meant the world to me. I recently found a photograph of the Princess talking to Wayne backstage after the performance. I took a close look and could make out an image of me, behind them, as you looked directly between them. It made me smile.

After the show, George, Wayne's manager, insisted on taking me and my family to The Ritz to have a final cheer together. It was a happy coincidence that this memorable evening took place where I had my first meeting with Anne Beckwith-Smith, who told me that the Princess wanted to dance, and that I would be her dancing teacher.

CHAPTER THIRTY-ONE

The Last Class

OUR LAST CLASS together began in the same way that our first class had begun, with the warm-up. I had never altered the basics of the warm-up but did it at a faster pace, along with more challenging leg extensions and holding positions, since Diana's body now knew the techniques and could work with them.

The lady that stood across from me these many years later stood tall, her head beautifully poised, shoulders down and relaxed; she was filled with a serene confidence that gave me great joy. She now looked me straight in the eye, her eyes shining. We both knew that we shared something unique. A special bond had been created between us because of Diana's love of dance. We went through our routine in an air of mutual respect for the movement, with that ineffable feeling of being alive.

I was leaving a very different lady to the very innocent one I had first met. I had enjoyed the privilege of witnessing nine years of growth in Diana. At times her challenges were daunting, but she had found the courage to overcome so many of them. The biggest, keeping her marriage, was still to be determined, but this new Diana was now capable of discerning what was best for herself and her children. She would no longer be a victim, but chose to embrace her role as Princess of Wales with all that she had, taking her own direction.

I felt confident I was leaving someone who was going to be in control of her life, which gave me solace. Like Diana, I would miss our time together, dreadfully, but knew I really didn't have a choice, and so appreciated her understanding and acceptance with such grace of this very big decision in my life.

Our goodbye was sweet, with us both saying we were not going to cry. Diana told me that she had ordered something special for me, which wasn't ready yet, but she would have it sent to me. The gift arrived at my Glasgow address some weeks later. It was a silver pair of miniature ballet shoes that she had specially made by Freed of London's ballet shop. Her note that came filled my heart:

The enclosed comes with all my love and heartfelt thanks for your kindness and special friendship during the last few years.

I am going to miss you dreadfully but will always remember the fun we had!

CHAPTER THIRTY-TWO

Darling Daddy

THE NEXT YEAR brought a vast change to my life. There was no salvaging my marriage and I found myself a single parent with three children.

At the same time, I was offered a permanent position in Toronto, as resident director with Garth Drabinsky's theatrical production company, Livent. It seemed a gift handed to me. Although it would be hard to leave my Scottish family, I knew it was a golden opportunity. My darling mum came with me for the first few weeks in the summer of 1990 to help settle us into our new life. My children, who now were two, four, and twelve, enjoyed the fact that there were warm summers and, since we were living in an area of Toronto called the Beaches, we had only to take a short walk to Lake Ontario to enjoy the sands. The snowy, cold winters were a delight, too, at least for first timers, with sledding down hills and throwing snowballs.

Time passed very quickly. I spent many hours on *Phantom,* as it is nicknamed, and mounting a Canadian tour company for *Phantom* after conducting many auditions and casting it with a Canadian cast. When I wasn't working, I was at home with my children, wanting to see them every minute that I could.

By 1992, *Phantom* was in its third year at the magnificent Pantages Theatre with the outstanding voice of Colm Wilkinson thrilling audiences. The Canadian touring company was meanwhile on the road, and I was into rehearsals for a daring new production of an original musical, *Kiss of the Spider Woman*.

It was the end of March that year and a Sunday. I loved Sundays, our family days, the days off after our very busy weeks. I was relaxing with the kids playing around me and watching television, when a news flash announced the death of the 8th Earl Spencer, Diana's father. My immediate thought was of her. I knew she would be heartbroken. According to the news, he had passed away following a heart attack after being admitted to hospital with pneumonia. The Princess was on holiday in Austria, skiing with her husband and the boys, and would be returning to London immediately. What made this so sad was that she and William had visited her father in hospital just before they went away. I knew she must have thought that all would be okay, which would deepen the pain of his sudden passing. I knew she would be distraught, and I wanted desperately to reach out to her.

Her relationship with her father hadn't always been good, but any time she spoke to me about him, it was always with love. Diana had told me that, although her father knew she was in love with Charles, he was worried about her marrying into "The Firm." His family had been a part of the British aristocracy for centuries. He himself had been an equerry to the late King George VI and also to the late Queen Elizabeth II. Diana said he had voiced concerns about her marrying into the demanding royal life. Despite the effects of a stroke in 1978 that had weakened him physically, the world watched him courageously walk his daughter down the aisle that memorable day in 1981.

Diana had affectionately joked with me a few times that "if *darling daddy* runs out of money, he just sells another painting." Apparently, he had quite a collection of works by the seventeenth-century Fleming artist Anthony van Dyck.

She was very much on my mind over the next couple of days. I saw the footage of the funeral, my heart heavy for her. Losing a parent is very difficult and I wanted to try and reach her, to let her know how much I was thinking about her.

I still had the telephone number that I had formerly used to contact her directly. Diana had given it to me some years before. I never wanted to abuse the privilege. Her time was precious and we'd done most of our chatting in the dance studio, sitting on the floor. I had only called a few times, and she had occasionally called me, or left a message saying, "Please tell Anne that Diana called."

It had been some time since we had been in touch. There is almost an unsaid understanding that once your time is complete with a royal and your duties finished, you don't hear from them anymore. I never expected to. However, my time with the Princess had been unique, and we had developed a friendship. I thought to myself, *if this were any other friend, I would pick up the phone without thinking*. So, I decided to do just that.

I dialed the number, unsure I would get any answer. A sweet voice at the other end said "Hello." I immediately said, "Hello Diana, this is Anne calling from Toronto." I wanted to make sure she knew it was me, although with my Scottish accent, I wasn't difficult to identify. "Oh Anne, I might have known it would be you," she said. I was touched. I told her how much I was thinking of her and how sad I was for her on her father's passing. "You know me so well, Anne. I'm heartbroken. Thank you for keeping me in your thoughts; it has been very difficult." We talked a little. The conversation led me to asking how things were going. Diana knew exactly what I meant, and answered with, "Nothing changes, Anne, nothing changes."

There was a complete understanding between us of what those words conveyed, and none of it was to be discussed over the phone. After a few more minutes and a fond farewell, Diana said, "Please call again, Anne," and I put the phone down.

I was sad, remembering how hopeful Diana had been when I left the U.K. for Canada. She was confident that *the new her* would be able to conquer and find a way forward with her marriage. I could tell this wouldn't be the case from the tone in her voice.

CHAPTER THIRTY-THREE

The Phone Call

AVING PROMISED DIANA that I would telephone again, I picked up the phone and dialed Diana's number a few weeks later. I wanted to see how she was doing in the wake of her darling daddy's passing. I dialed the same number I had previously called. The telephone line was dead.

I was bewildered. How could it be that Diana's private telephone number no longer existed? There was no ring. Just a flat low tone, an eternal nothingness. It was upsetting, and I felt sure that something deliberate had happened. I did not think it was Diana's doing. She wouldn't have said please call again if she had known.

In our last conversation, there was unspoken recognition of ongoing problems for Diana, and although she was grieving, I knew her well enough to know that the marriage was not going well.

There had been commentary in the news suggesting that the Prince and Princess of Wales were completely distant from one another. The photographs on their six-day visit to India in February 1992 seemed to tell the obvious story. Charles and Diana were often seen looking off in different directions; their body language spoke volumes. Diana was captured sitting alone in front of the Taj Mahal, looking pensive and solitary. Although the moment could have been perceived as a thoughtful moment in respect to the majestic building behind her, it was read as a deliberate statement from Diana of how alone she felt. Many considered that Diana had staged the moment. It may well have been so. By this time, Diana had been married for more than ten years and possibly was unable to hide the relentless hurt any longer. I felt devastated on her behalf. I had been so hopeful for the stunning, strong lady I had seen at our last dance class in 1989. I firmly believed that she had found a new inner strength and conviction and that these qualities would help her move forward.

I sat thinking through the possible reasons for the phone being dead. Now I had no way of reaching Diana and I wasn't sure that she had my number.

There was nothing I could do.

The Andrew Morton book was released in June 1992. Diana had finally found a way to use her voice and had given herself the right to speak her truth. I know she would have wrestled with the decision and the serious damage that would be done by speaking out, but I believe she had been pushed to the brink and saw no way out if she did not come clean. She was expected to live as though she and Charles were in a marriage when, in fact, they were living separate lives, just to uphold the reputation for the monarchy. It was only possible at the expense of her well-being. How many years of unhappiness and dishonesty does one have to suffer before concluding that things have got to change?

I did not rush out to buy the book. I could surmise from the conversations that had taken place between us what it would contain. When years later I picked up a copy, I found I wasn't wrong. I remained concerned for Diana. I wasn't sure exactly how things would play out for her.

The official separation of the Prince and Princess of Wales was announced six months later, on December 9, 1992.

CHAPTER THIRTY-FOUR

Serendipity

IN JULY OF the following year, 1993, I was back in London to check on the production of the musical we had mounted, *Kiss of the Spider Woman*. It had opened the previous October at the Shaftsbury Theatre in London's West End. The Tony Awards had just taken place in New York City. The show won eleven awards, including best musical. Chita Rivera, who originated *Anita* in *West Side Story*, *Velma* in *Chicago* now a Broadway legend who we lost in January 30 2024, played Spider Woman and won best actress. In her lifetime she won many awards including the Presidential Medal of Freedom and a Kennedy Center Honor but she always described herself as a dancer first. The brilliant Canadian Brent Carver (who passed away in 2020), won best actor for his portrayal of one of the main characters, Molina. Terrence McNally (who also passed away in 2020) won best writer.

I had so admired how Terrence crafted this complex subject from the book by Argentine author Manuel Puig (1932–1990) into a musical about Argentina in the 1970s. It is quite unlike any other musical and anything but a happy, lighthearted fantasy. It is a gritty drama dealing with real life, politics, and revolution, and contains themes of escapism and brutality, both physical and mental. Hal Prince, with his fearless determination that musicals should do more than entertain, saw the opportunity to bring attention to human rights violations by creating *Kiss of the Spider Woman*.

The story takes place in a prison, where Molina is a cellmate to the revolutionary Valentin, played by Anthony Crivello (who won for best actor in a feature role), and is trying to prevent Valentin from cracking under pressure. To do so, Molina vividly recounts his memories of his favourite Technicolor movies. These scenes lend themselves to inspired choreography by Rob Marshall (who won for best choreography). The power and impact of the original score by the dynamic duo John Kander and Fred Ebb, who won for best original score, was obvious. Audiences would get to their feet in appreciation of hearing the uplifting anthem, "The Day After That."

The awards meant a great deal to the artistic team and everyone who had worked on the show, especially those who had launched the risky venture. Producer Garth Drabinsky had believed in the show's importance and ultimate success from the beginning. He had smartly opened it first in Toronto at the Bluma Appel Theatre in the St. Lawrence Centre for the Arts, and then at the Shaftesbury Theatre in London's West End, where it won the Drama Desk Award for best musical, which helped to pave its way to Broadway.

I was excited to be back in London again and to see the new cast, including Bebe Neuwirth playing Spider Woman. I was also able to catch up with family and friends.

I had finished rehearsals and watched a few shows to make sure that any notes I had given had been incorporated. On the day off, Sunday, I gave George Lawson, Wayne's manager, a call. I hadn't seen Wayne or

George since before I'd left for Canada, but I knew if he had some time, we would reconnect.

George answered the phone right away saying, "Anne, how lovely, such serendipity! Wayne is performing tomorrow night in a gala that the Princess of Wales is officially attending. Please come!" I could hardly believe it. Perfect timing. I very happily agreed, thanking him for organizing the ticket on such short notice.

The black-tie gala was in honour of the reopening of the newly refurbished Savoy Theatre. A 1990 fire had caused extensive damage to the interior and destroyed the Art Deco design. Fortunately, the fire did not spread to the Savoy Hotel next door, and no one was hurt.

An additional surprise for me was that the English National Ballet was to perform that evening. Diana was now patron of the company, in addition to being patron of the London City Ballet. The English National Ballet rehearsal studios were where we had held our dance classes. Wayne had been commissioned to create a ballet for the gala, which he called *Savoy Suite*. It was inspired by the music of Gilbert and Sullivan and was to honour the legacy of their history with the D'Oyly Carte Opera Company, which had first performed in the Savoy Theatre in 1881.

It was a wonderful, glittering affair. The Princess looked dazzling and happy in a pale-pink jewelled dress. Now that she was separated from Charles, she appeared to be thriving, which gave me great joy. I knew that it was an official opening and her schedule would be jammed with dignitaries to meet, and there would be little to no chance of seeing her face-to-face or getting to say hello. I didn't mind, although it felt perhaps bittersweet. I was looking forward to seeing Wayne for drinks after the performance.

When Wayne, George, and I finally connected, Wayne told me that he had managed to have a short conversation with Diana, as she made her way down the backstage presentation line following the performance. He had told her I was in London and attending the gala. She had responded warmly, he said, as she was ushered further down the line. I was touched at his thoughtfulness to make sure Diana knew I was there, especially after dancing at such an important event and with his adrenalin still pumping. It was admirable.

A couple of days later, I arrived back at my hotel to pack and, as I was leaving, the front-desk clerk passed me a telephone message. It read: "Park Plaza Hotel 22/7/93: Diana telephoned."

I wasn't sure how she'd got the number, but George did know that I was staying at that hotel. Diana must have had her office inquire and had taken the time to call me directly. It was unfortunate that I was not there when she called, but my heart was full, knowing she had been in touch.

Later that year, on December 3, Diana announced that she was stepping back from the duties of public life to focus on what she hoped would be a more meaningful public role and a more private life. Finally, her life would be her own. I felt more complete knowing that she was moving forward with such confidence.

CHAPTER THIRTY-FIVE

Shock

TIME PASSED. ALTHOUGH Diana, whose divorce was finalized in 1996, had asked for a more private life, the press continued to stalk her, detailing everything from her crusade against land mines to any instance that she was seen with a new man in her life. It must have been trying for her.

In Toronto, I was anticipating the closing night of the musical *Ragtime* after a very successful run at the Ford Centre for the Performing Arts. The excitement of the cast was palpable; its members knew the show was headed for Broadway.

Playing Broadway was, and still is, the epitome of success for a show. It also meant that the Americans in the cast got to go home knowing they had a potential hit show on their hands.

It had been another miraculous journey to get the show this far. Garth Drabinsky was again the producer, and had taken the risk of mounting a complex musical, based on the 1975 novel by E.L. Doctorow, with a very large cast of forty.

The opening lines are spoken by the little boy, Edgar: "In 1902, father built a house at the crest of the Broadview Avenue hill in New Rochelle,

New York, and it seemed for some years thereafter that all the family's days would be warm and fair." These words, which also serve as the introduction to the novel, foreshadow the radically changing world about to unfold.

Ragtime deals with sharp contrasts of wealth and poverty, freedom and prejudice, hope and despair. It follows three diverse groups of Americans at the turn of the twentieth century, each in search of its version of the American Dream, and each depicted by a family with a central character. The upper-class white suburbanites are represented by Mother, played by the late and outstanding Marin Mazzie. The African Americans are represented by Coalhouse Walker Jr., played by Brian Stokes Mitchell, a professional musician living in Harlem and known for his performances of ragtime music. He falls in love with Sarah, played by the veteran Broadway star Audra McDonald, who ultimately won her first Tony Award for her role. The immigrant Jewish family is led by Tateh, played by Peter Friedman, and his young daughter, played by Lea Michele.

The musical also features factual characters from the period—J.P. Morgan, Harry Houdini, Henry Ford, Evelyn Nesbit, Emma Goldman, and Booker T. Washington—and shows the audience their influence on America at that time.

The late Terrence McNally brilliantly condensed Doctorow's epic book into a script for the musical, with Stephen Flaherty as the composer and Lynn Ahrens as the lyricist, an extraordinary musical force in their partnership. Frank Galati (who sadly passed away in January 2023) directed in his warm, teddy-bear style. His eloquence inspired every step of the way. The choreographer, Graciela Daniele, created ingenious, show-stopping numbers and told stories through movement while also solving staging problems. She had deeply researched immigrant life and felt a part of it, having arrived in New York City from Argentina. Gabriela was a remarkable woman who became a mentor to me at the time, and still is.

I wanted to share this very special night and the celebratory after-party at the Ford Centre theatre with my family, so I had booked a family room at the hotel next door. My kids were older now—Emily was twenty, Victoria twelve, and Alastair ten—and they loved this kind of outing. The hotel also had a swimming pool where they spent some time. The plan was that they would join me at the back of the auditorium at the end of the show to congratulate the cast and join the after-party for a bit.

After cheers and tremendous applause from the audience, sending the show off in great style, we made our way to the after-party. I had a chance to thank most people involved and was just rewarding myself with a glass of champagne when Stafford Arima, my associate on the show, came forward. I could see from his face that he was troubled. "Anne, I think you better go and see the news on television."

I looked at him completely bewildered. What was he talking about?

"There has been a terrible accident and someone you know has been hurt."

Still seeing the perplexed look on my face, he said, "It's Diana, the Princess."

I had shared with Stafford that I had spent some time with Diana. The subject had come up in 1996, when news of her divorce from Charles hit the headlines. He was aware of what she meant to me.

I was in a daze and couldn't quite take it in. I knew I needed to get out of that room as fast as I could. I found my daughter Emily, told her that I had to go to the hotel room, and asked her to bring Victoria and Alastair back in a few minutes. I flew by people who were still in party mode and made it to the elevator, which seemed to take an eternity. I finally arrived in our hotel room and switched on the television. The shock hit me. There had been a car accident in a tunnel in Paris and Diana was being taken to hospital.

I sat numb and in disbelief. Emily must have come in with the children. She was hugging me. Vicky and Alastair were sitting around. holding on to me. They knew I was distressed and said nothing, just sat with me. In time I was able to speak, and I asked them if it was all right if we just sat quietly together. Emily asked if I wanted to go straight home, but I didn't and couldn't. I was finding it hard to move.

I prayed that Diana was going to pull through, but I felt such heaviness in my heart. I knew I might be fooling myself. I sat up with Emily until news of her death was announced. Her life ended on August 31, 1997. Like the rest of the world, I was in total shock.

My first cohesive thoughts were of William and Harry. How do you tell two young people that they are never going to see their mother again? I sobbed for them. I also wept for Charles, who would suffer deeply, regardless of the divorce. The circumstances of the death were horrendous.

At some point, we must have all fallen asleep. The next morning, we made our way home. I was glad for my children to be back with their friends. I was completely depleted. I watched the coverage on television like a zombie and was interrupted with a phone call from my sisters in Glasgow, who knew I would be suffering. It made me think of Diana's sisters and her brother and what they must have been going through.

That call was the thing I needed most. With my family, I could share my personal grief and not feel alone. And, through the television coverage, I could see the reactions of others from around the world and the genuine sadness of everyday people who also felt so close to Diana as the People's Princess. So many were heartbroken. As I watched flowers being laid at Buckingham Palace by those who had come to pay tribute to her memory, I took comfort in the fact that she was so loved. The sea of flowers told its own story.

I remember being interviewed for a television documentary about Diana and being asked, "What do you think of the Queen's response to Diana's death and the fact that she stayed at Balmoral?" It was a distasteful question. The interviewer was looking for a negative response that could be sensationalized.

"No one can imagine what another person is feeling on the news of a death and Diana's must have been personally and publicly extremely difficult for the Queen," I said. "She had her grandchildren and her own son to think about. Who are we to question the Queen's choices or to begin to understand how she felt?"

On the day of her funeral, I joined millions of other people from around the world in watching the service and procession on television. Afterwards, I held my own private vigil at home, surrounding myself with candles, flowers, and Diana's dance photos and letters. All I could do was remember and cherish the time we had together. It helped to fill the emptiness I was feeling. I would need a fair bit of time over the next few months to come to terms with her death.

CHAPTER THIRTY-SIX

The Royal Visits

M Y PROFESSIONAL WORK continued, directing and choreographing across Canada. Between 2004 and 2014, I found myself as artistic director of the Charlottetown Festival at the Confederation Centre of the Arts on beautiful Prince Edward Island. Every year, I spent April to September there and the rest of the time in Toronto, allowing me to enjoy the best of both worlds. My now-grown children would come home for a visit or for opening nights when their schedules would allow. Emily was creating art, Victoria was a beautiful actor, and Alastair was coaching tennis.

P.E.I. is known for its white beaches, often called the "Singing Sands"— you hear a melodic sound when you walk on them. It also has red sand beaches coloured by the wealth of iron that has eroded over the years from the sandstone. The landscape was the inspiration for the iconic *Anne of Green Gables*, written by Lucy Maud Montgomery in 1908. The beloved book became a musical in 1965, written by Don Harron and Norman Campbell.

Don told me how the book became a musical. He and Norman had written a song for the inaugural opening of the Confederation Centre of the Arts by Queen Elizabeth II in 1964. When they met her, she had asked if she could come back and see the rest of the musical. The Queen's request inspired the duo to begin writing immediately; they considered the request a royal command. The full musical played the following year at the Charlottetown Festival and was performed on the stages of the Confederation Centre.

From its first performance, it was a great success and has played every year since, barring the year of the COVID-19 pandemic. Tourists come from around the world especially to visit the place where "Anne with an e" was created, to take in the beautiful landscape, and to see this beloved character on stage. I was honoured to direct it for many years.

The Confederation Centre of the Arts is a National Historic Site and a memorial to the Fathers of Confederation. Its intention was best described by Prime Minister Lester B. Pearson, who attended its inauguration on October 6, 1964: "The Fathers of Confederation Memorial Building is a tribute to those famous men who founded our Confederation. But it is also dedicated to the fostering of those things that enrich the mind and delight the heart, those intangible but precious things that give meaning to a society and help create from it a civilization and a culture."

In the summer of 2011, everyone at the Confederation Centre was thrilled to learn that a royal visit would be made by the newly married Duke and Duchess of Cambridge, a.k.a. William and Kate, as part of their nine-day trip to Canada. I was excited by the possibility of meeting Diana's son, then twenty-nine years old. I thought it would be wonderful to describe for him the joy with which she had always spoken of her sons, and how beautiful she was to me.

I forwarded a note to him, along with one of the letters I had received from Diana (for authenticity), through official channels in hopes that it would reach him. Of course, I knew that Their Royal Highnesses' schedules would be extremely busy. It was an official tour, with every detail of the visit carefully planned and overseen with precise timing by officials from the Palace and the team travelling with them. Every bit of protocol and etiquette would have been discussed in detail ahead of the visit. It is a well-oiled machine.

On the day of the visit, I was among those scheduled to greet the couple at Confederation Centre, in my capacity as artistic director of the festival. I think everyone in Charlottetown was out on the streets that day, including children waving flags or holding the posters made to welcome the future king and queen and do them proud, as they say on the Island. The Duke and Duchess of Cambridge arrived in an open-top carriage escorted by the Mounties in their vivid red uniforms, a magnificent sight. They both looked relaxed and happy, Kate wearing a knee-length cream skirt and matching top with a nautical feel. She was very beautiful.

My heart was beating fast as they made their way down the line. As William approached, I wondered whether or not I should say anything to him and decided to seize the moment. He shook my hand warmly and after he had spoken, I blurted out that I had had the privilege of teaching his mother dancing back in London. "How nice," he replied, and moved on. That was it.

It must have seemed to Prince William that I was a bit of a mad woman—he obviously hadn't received the letter and he would have had no way of knowing of my relationship with his mother. I knew from her how often random comments were thrown at them in public. I was nevertheless a bit disappointed that I hadn't been able to tell him of those treasured times and Diana's joy when she spoke about him.

The next royal visit to Charlottetown was scheduled for 2014. This time it was to be Prince Charles with his wife Camilla, whom he had married in 2005. I had found it difficult to watch that wedding. I knew what Diana had suffered. Even though she was no longer with us, and Charles had every right to happiness, it stabbed at my very being.

The last time Prince Charles had been in P.E.I. was in 1983 with Diana. I remembered it vividly because it was one of Diana's first overseas tours. Now, he would be coming for his second visit, this time as a grandfather to William's infant son, Prince George.

The occasion for the visit to Charlottetown was a celebration of the 150th anniversary of the meeting of the Fathers of Confederation, which had led to Canada's Confederation in 1867. On their first evening, the royals were to attend an outdoor concert featuring an abundance of P.E.I. talent, with robust storytelling through music and sensational step dancing. Even the rain that night could not dampen the enthusiasm of the performers or the audience.

The following day, Charles and Camilla were to make their way to Memorial Hall in the Confederation Centre, where he was to receive an honorary Symons Medal for his contribution to Canadian society and say a few words. I was to be part of the congratulatory receiving line. I was dreading it, but did not make my feelings evident to anyone—it was my duty as artistic director to attend and I certainly wasn't going to be rude to the Prince on his special occasion.

I was just about to head to the centre when I received a phone call from one of my cast members. I knew from the tone of her voice that it was bad news. And it was. Val Hawkins, a cast member with an incredible voice, had just received a shocking diagnosis of ovarian cancer. Val had wanted to tell me straight away, as it would mean missing performances. She had asked this cast member to deliver the news.

I was devastated for Val. What had seemed to be a very bad cough with the loss of her voice had turned out to be cancer. I knew in my heart that ovarian cancer would not have a happy outcome. It was appalling and unbelievable. I immediately suggested that both Val and the cast member come to my apartment so we could be together and figure out the best way to deal with this news. The three of us had known one another for many years and were close friends. We sat together and talked. Amid the myriad of emotions, I knew it was important for me to stay there. I telephoned the Confederation Centre to say that, regrettably, I would not be able to attend the function for Prince Charles.

CHAPTER THIRTY-SEVEN

The Reporter

I WAS APPROACHED TO do an interview for a six-part original TV documentary by CNN titled *The Windsors: Inside the Royal Dynasty*. Since CNN was a reputable organization that had good work with *American Dynasties: The Kennedys*, I had some hope that it might be handled well. The production company, Raw TV, was based in London. Charles Colville was the producer.

After some emails back and forth, a Zoom conversation was arranged. Charles made a compelling pitch that seemed authentic in style and intention. He hoped that the viewers would find the series both enlightening and insightful and see a true portrait of Diana, unlike anything done before. I expressed my reticence, but on his assurance that his intention was to document the truth from people who knew Diana and that it would not be in any way derogatory, I was persuaded to do it. This was 2019 and I partly felt it might finally be time to tell some of my personal stories to bring further insight into Diana's life in a positive way.

In September, the company flew me from New York, where I was at the time, to London for the interview. I enjoyed being back in London, even for a short stay. The day before the interview, I visited Hyde Park to see the Diana, Princess of Wales Memorial Fountain. It is a beautiful circular structure designed by Gustafson Porter. Built from Cornish granite, it has water flowing in two directions, creating swirling bubbles, and a gentle, calm flow. The contrasts were intended to reflect Diana's life. It was very reflective for me and served as an inspiration for the interview.

The atmosphere on filming day was respectful and congenial. There was a small crew for camera, lights, and make-up touch-ups. The interview lasted several hours, longer than I had expected, but there appeared to be genuine interest as I talked about Diana's love of dance, the circumstances of the class, and the fun times we had together.

Charles was a good interviewer and instantly likeable. Like any good documentarian, he began to probe, as time went by, into the demise of Charles and Diana's marriage, and asked some other personal questions about Diana. I wasn't willing to say much on those subjects. He did, however, get several hours of footage. I returned home to Canada feeling that the interview had gone well.

A few days later, I was returning from my local shops, bags in hand, to the coach house where I lived. Much like the mews where Wayne had lived in London, it was behind the main house, almost hidden, and had two levels. As I was approaching the front entrance, I saw a gentleman hovering nearby. He smiled as I went by. I made my way to my private entrance and went up the stairs to drop the heavy shopping bags in the kitchen. I'd left the door open as I went upstairs, as I often do—my home wasn't visible from the street and neither was the small patio outside, where I loved to sit, surrounded by flowers.

There was a rapid knock on the door as I was putting the shopping away. I heard someone shout, "Hello, Hello!" I came to the top of the stairs and the man I had seen outside apologized if he had startled me.

I noticed he had an English accent. He said he was looking for Anne Allan and thought it might be me. As I made my way downstairs, he said, "I've been sent by the documentary company to see you. I've just arrived from the airport."

It seemed logical—I had just returned a few days earlier from filming. I presumed that Charles may have still needed something. I invited the man in for tea, as we Scots do. He was most grateful as he had just flown in from New York.

"New York?" I asked.

"Yes," he said, "that's where I was when I got the call to come and see you."

I made tea in the kitchen, keeping an eye on him in the living room. The man was looking around. He saw a photograph of Diana and Wayne dancing that I kept on a shelf, behind the glass door of a cabinet. I quickly brought in the tea and politely asked him to sit on the couch.

We made a few exchanges about traffic from the airport, and he started to ask questions about Diana and my time as her dancing teacher. He was smiling and inquisitive. I was a bit suspicious, but did not want to be rude. I said that the film company already had a lot of the information from the interview. He nodded, then continued asking questions.

I finally asked, "Who is it that sent you, again?"

"The film company."

That put me on my guard. I let him sip some tea then asked exactly what was needed. I watched him flounder with his response. Then came the bombshell.

"Actually, I'm a reporter and wanted to ask you if you would do an interview."

Keeping outwardly calm, I declined the offer. Internally, I was thinking, *how the hell can I get him out of here?* A tabloid newspaper had sent him. There had been an article advertising the upcoming documentary where my name was mentioned; that's how he knew who I was.

I thought it best to remain congenial. I thanked him for the request and let him know that I was not doing any press interviews of any kind regarding the documentary. He tried to push it a bit, but I stood up and ushered him downstairs. He thanked me for the tea and apologized for the inconvenience. I shut the door and locked it, shaken.

I texted my son, who was living close by, to come round. Alastair arrived within minutes. I knew his six-foot, five-inch stature would be forbidding if the reporter was still hanging about. My son and I both sat with a large Scotch to calm me down. I was in disbelief at the lengths reporters would go to for a story. It was the tiniest taste of what it must have been like for Diana.

The documentary finally aired in 2020, and although it successfully captured the lengthy history of the House of Windsor's dynasty and was insightful for a lot of viewers, I was deeply disappointed. The tiny segment of my contribution on Diana dealt only with the marriage, with a snippet on her love of dance. The true portrait of Diana, as promised by Charles Colville, was not evident to me.

That was when the seed was planted in my mind to write my story.

Curtain Call

"WHO'S THAT, NANA?" asked my three-year-old granddaughter, Siena, as she looked at a photograph in her little hands. She had managed to take the picture of Diana and Wayne dancing from the shelf after opening the cabinet—"all by myself, Nana," she told me proudly.

"That is the Princess," I said, smiling.

"A princess," she repeated with wide eyes.

"Yes," I said. "Princess Diana. She loved to dance."

"I like dancing too," she told me.

"Do you know a princess, Nana?" she asked, looking at me inquisitively.

I showed Siena a photo of the Princess taking a final bow in the curtain call after her performance at Covent Garden in 1985, sparking in me a flood of memories.

"Yes, I did, but it was a long time ago," I said. "Shall I tell you about her?"

"Yes, please, Nana."

So, I told her and, shortly after that evening, at the beginning of 2023, I actually sat down to write this book. It has been an emotional roller coaster. I hope, more than anything, that it has communicated Diana's love of dance and brought a deeper understanding of the very human side of Diana, while attesting to how extraordinary she was.

My wise and wonderful first editor, Beth McAuley, in one of our meetings asked me, "How do you manage to hold all this in?" It was an intelligent and sensitive question. I was touched, as no one had asked before. The truth is that it wasn't easy at times. To hold in yourself the feelings expressed to you, unable to do anything concrete to help, particularly as Diana was going through her difficulties, often left me with a very heavy heart.

But my fondest memories of Diana are of her profound love of dance, which was always a joy to feel and see. Dance was a beautiful passion and outlet for her. Dance, with its freedom of movement, reveals its own language, an expression of true feeling—"the emotion in motion." For Diana, it nourished and renewed her soul. In her own words, "Dancing makes you feel heaps better."

That is what dance was to Diana. In our classes, she was nothing but her true self. Dance allowed the light within her to burn brighter, and I was given the extraordinary honour of being a part of it.

And so, Diana, as you take your curtain call, you deserve to be loudly applauded. Thank you.

Acknowledgements

I N BETWEEN CHAPTERS, I have enjoyed many beautiful walks to the beach and in surrounding parks, my mind filled with gratitude, thankful for the love and support that has surrounded me as I wrote this book.

My thanks must begin with the privilege of knowing Diana and my appreciation of our time together, talking and sharing our love of dance.

I met my first editor, Beth McAuley of The Editing Company, when Cynthia Goode, a publishing consultant introduced to me by my friend Debra Bennett, advised me that I needed a good editor. From the first phone call and in all subsequent meetings, Beth listened intently as I explained the intention of the book, responding with "I love that you are sharing this story with the world." She understood how daunting it is to pass your work over for comment when no one else has read it. Her encouragement and wisdom as she worked through every page of the first draft was remarkable. I will always be grateful to Beth for her understanding and excellent work.

Finding a publisher for a first-time writer can be challenging. I was lucky that Garth Drabinsky, who gave me positive affirmation that the book was a good idea, had a chance meeting with Ken Whyte of Sutherland

House Books. They had worked together in the past, including when Garth produced the celebration of the centenary of Maclean's magazine, which I had helped with artistically. Garth, knowing the importance of a good publisher, went out of his way to speak to Ken on my behalf. My thanks to Garth for his assistance and all the creative conversations we have had over the years.

Ken, who knew little about me, invited me to meet and on the conclusion of our meeting, when asked him if he was interested in the book, replied yes, *very* interested! In that moment, my heart danced with appreciation. Ken has guided me through the publishing process with deep respect, giving his time, editing brilliance, and sensitivity to help me express everything I wanted to say. I am so grateful to him.

Thanks also to Ken's exceptional team at Sutherland House: Shalomi Ranasinghe, managing editor; Lena Yang, design director; Serina Mercier, marketing director; Leah Ciani, editorial assistant; and Sarah Miniaci, publicist. Their creative minds contributed to a vastly better publishing experience.

I would be lost without the help of me agents, including my friend and advisor over many years, Bruce Dean of The Talent House, and the singular, superb Michael Petrasek, my literary agent, who is always intuitive and makes me feel confident that I am in excellent hands.

My thanks to Wayne Sleep and Karen Kain for immediately agreeing to endorse the book.

Heartfelt thanks to my trio of true friends for their unconditional care, and trust: Beth Russell, my confidante for years, just retired as casting director of the Stratford Shakespeare Festival (it was Beth who helped me land the title of the book); Debra Bennett, a published poet and an incredible estate agent, for her intellect, recommendations, and humor; and Sandy Pearl, a media and art consultant and a writer herself, who sat through conversations over lunch as I poured out my thoughts and gave me further incentive and reassurance.

When I told my eldest sister Georgina, who sadly has dementia, that I was writing this book, she took me by the hand and said, "Darling, I'm your big sister, good, I knew you would do it." That moment of lucidity and love gave me strength. Georgina has always been my shining light.

A special thanks to my sister, Feona, who has been there through every step of my life, who never revealed my time with the princess to anyone, and who was always willing to lend an ear and help me.

My two Scottish nieces, Alex and Becca, said "we're proud of you, Auntie," words that meant the world to me. They acted as their darling mum would have; my dear sister, Rebecca, passed away a few years ago. Becky's husband, my brother-in-law, Jim, is my constant supporter. Thank you, also, to all of my family in the UK, who have promised a few wee drams on the next visit, and to my great nephew, Harvey, who is now a dancer with Scottish Ballet, continuing the family legacy of loving dance.

Lastly, but most importantly, thanks to my immediate family members for their endless support, love, care, and laughter as they journeyed through "mother's writing a book!" You are my life and my joy. Thank you, Emily, for cementing my belief in the importance of the book; Victoria for dealing with my endless texts, phone calls, and creative discussions as I was writing, always offering her insightful, intelligent, responses and suggestions, dipped in love; Alastair, whose loyalty and lasting encouragement were there whenever I needed them; Lexie, my daughter-in-law, who kept the excitement alive; and my stepdaughter, Celine, who listened intently to every bit of the process with a beaming smile.

Finally, to my darling grand-daughter Siena. Thank you. You are my inspiration.

HIGHGROVE

August: 6th
1988.

Dearest Anne,

I couldn't be more thrilled with the video & how I laugh every time I see the credits!

It was a wonderful opportunity for me to have the dance filmed & now its on record! ☺

Needless to say, I see alot of mistakes as do William & Harry who have great enjoyment pointing out Mummy with her head down or 'why aren't you smiling'!

The team you organised for our morning were terrific — I dread to think what they thought of it all, this sweaty female leaping about!

It was typical of you to have sent me the wonderful card — you always know how to bring a smile to my face —

HIGHGROVE

I hated cancelling our lesson for Tuesday, but with the boys here it was difficult to up & go —

However, I hope you have a well earned rest, whether it be from Gay bars in Madrid or exhausted females like me!

Take care Anne & all my love & thanks for everything, from Diana.

KENSINGTON PALACE

August: 6th
1986.

Dearest Anne,

I could not go to bed without putting pen to paper to thank you both so much for organising my night out on the town!

I had the most wonderful evening with lots of laughter & fun & how marvellous it